Advance praise for
BEYOND STRATEGY—THE LEAL
SUCCESSFUL IMPLEMEN1

Many books have been written about how to create a winning strategy. And to-day, many more books are written on the importance of strategy implementation. Leaders understand a strategy is only effective when it is implemented successfully. This book is written for those leaders who must implement a strategy and need to know: "What must I do differently? What must I do now? What new actions are required?" When you are serious about business success, you must go *Beyond Strategy* to achieve effective strategy implementation. You must read and apply what you learn in this book. Good luck!

Ron Kaufman
CEO and Founder, UP Your Service! College

I have worked with Robin on and off for 10 years and his message to leaders is simple, clear and logical, and I encourage readers of this book to accept the message and run with it. When you talk to people about strategy most of them start dreaming of the future, market sizing, blue oceans, and emotional intelligence. When you talk to Robin, he asks "How are you going to implement it?" I, like most leaders, have been guilty of overpromising and under-delivering. If you follow Robin's compass relentlessly and are prepared for the hard work it entails, you will over-deliver.

Andrew Duff
General Manager, International Banking, QNB

As Robin points out in the book, implementation may not be near as attractive as creating strategy, but it is far more important. If you're a leader who wants to ensure successful implementation, this book is for you. You'll never take execution for granted again as you learn to effectively implement strategy. Why waste money creating strategy that's not implemented, when for a tiny investment, you'll learn the way to do it right. A must read!

Scott Friedman, CSP
Motivational Humorist
President, National Speakers Association

Robin's got this topic spot on! In my experience working with multinationals, senior leaders rarely get involved in implementation, assuming that is not part of their role. In Robin's book, he clearly identifies a process and actions that leaders need to take to ensure the success of their business strategy. Significant change is not easy, and if employees do not get the sense that senior managers are willing to work hard at it personally, they often will not embrace the change. A must-read for all senior leaders and others responsible for business strategy and its implementation!

James Dale
Principal, Hewitt Associates

Finally, a step-by-step guide on the "successful" implementation of strategy, Robin has lifted the veil on this complex and often misunderstood essential leadership task in a simple, concise way, enabling leaders at all levels to gain valuable insight into why so many strategies fail to deliver the desired outcome, challenging conventional "thinking" into "doing" through solid relevant global experience and real-life accounts, *Beyond Strategy* is an action-packed chronicle of best practices and thought-provoking situations combining to deliver a truly gripping journey as dynamic as global markets themselves.

John Griffiths
Country President, Schneider Electric Gulf Countries

Beyond Strategy boldly challenges the reader with the potential to fail once a perfect strategy has been devised and agreed by senior leaders. It provides innovative tools to maximize the chance of successful strategy implementation and is a pertinent reminder to all of us seeking excellence in leadership, people, change and mindset. Future success stories in the global economy will be led by those who think and act differently when they execute their strategy.

Hanno Ellensohn
Managing Director, K3 Performance Ltd.

Nobody has described strategy implementation better than Robin Speculand over the last 10 years. He has done it again with his new book by targeting the leader's role. This book is a practical approach that reduces complex material to easily understandable actions. I love the Implementation Compass that outlines the global best practices on successful implementation. This is a must-have book for every leader who needs to deliver on their strategy promise.

R. Palan Ph.D. A.P.T.
Chairman & CEO, SMR HR Technologies

Beyond Strategy

The Leader's Role in
Successful Implementation

Beyond Strategy

The Leader's Role in Successful Implementation

ROBIN SPECULAND

JOSSEY-BASS
A Wiley Imprint
www.josseybass.com

Jossey-Bass books and products are available through most bookstores. To contact Jossey-Bass directly call our Customer Care Department within the U.S. at 800-956-7739, outside the U.S. at 317-572-3986, or fax 317-572-4002.

Jossey-Bass also publishes its books in a variety of electronic formats. Some content that appears in print may not be available in electronic books.

Library of Congress Cataloging-in-Publication Data

ISBN: 978-0-470-82498-6

Typeset in 10.5/13pt Sabon by Aptara Inc., New Delhi, India.
Printed in Singapore

10 9 8 7 6 5 4 3 2 1

The best-laid schemes o' mice an' men/Gang aft a-gley.
(The most careful plans of mice and men often fail.)
—Robert Burns, "To a Mouse"

CONTENTS

INTRODUCTION

L eaders appreciate and understand that it is just as tough (if not tougher) to implement a great strategy as it is to craft it. Strategy implementation has become a discussion topic in board rooms and among leaders around the world, due to its staggering high failure rate.

The field is evolving and in *Beyond Strategy,* I move from building leaders awareness of the strategy implementation challenge—which was the focus of my last book *Bricks to Bridges: Make Your Strategy Come Alive*, published in 2004, to addressing specifically the leader's role in successful implementation. At the core of this role is the need to for leaders to recognize that traditional attitudes, approaches, and actions are a major factor behind these dismal results. To improve the chances of success, leaders must change what they have been doing in the past.

The oft-quoted observation in the 1999 *Fortune* magazine cover story, "Why CEOs Fail," explained, "Organizations fail to successfully implement strategy not because of bad strategy but because of bad execution."[1] This was one of the first times the field of implementation (the terms *execution* and *implementation* are interchangeable) received major exposure. In 2002, Ram Charan followed up the article by teaming up with Larry Bossidy to write *Execution: The Discipline of Getting Things Done,* the book that made *execution* a common word in mainstream business.[2] Since its publication, leaders have begun to focus on the topic, and a growing number of books and articles have followed. In 2004, *Bricks to Bridges* has gone on to be described as a handbook for leaders in implementing strategy, and has become an international best seller and a university supplementary textbook.

There still, however, exits a vast gap of knowledge, techniques, and tools in the field. For contrast, consider the plethora of tools and techniques available for crafting strategy: hundreds and even thousands of books on the topic, and consultants in every city standing by to offer leaders their support and wisdom. Despite the general understanding of strategy and how to create it, it is worth noting that even this is still a work in progress: we do not have a globally common definition for the word *strategy*.

But a change is in the wind. Leaders get it. They know they must pay greater attention to the implementation and that it is not the strategy that delivers revenue, it is its successful implementation. The question many are asking is, "What do we need to do different to succeed?" This is the focus of the book.

Professor Joseph Bower of the Harvard Business School recently said, "One of the *criticisms* we would have of some of our colleagues who have studied strategy (and some consultants who advise on strategy) is that they *assume* that once you design strategy, it gets executed. They don't look inside the process and realize that it's much more complicated."[3]

In this book, I aim to address the current void in the field and provide the techniques and tools for leaders to deliver on the promise of increasing shareholder value by executing their organizations' strategy. In each chapter, I highlight what leaders need to do differently. I challenge many of the conventional beliefs of business, and provide the framework of the Implementation Compass™ that I first published in *Bricks to Bridges*. The eight best global practices from the Compass serve as chapter headings. I focus solely on what actions leaders must take in the process, and each chapter ends with a summary called "Leaders' Role in Implementation." For a copy of the "Leaders' Role in Implementation" summaries, e-mail your request to bridges@bridgesconsultancy.com.

I wish you all the success on your implementation journey.

Robin Speculand
July 2009

Endnotes

1 Ram Charan and Geoffrey Colvin, "Why CEOs Fail: It's rarely for lack of smarts or vision. Most unsuccessful CEOs stumble because of one simple, fatal shortcoming," *Fortune,* June 21, 1999, p. 68; accessed at http://money.cnn.

com/magazines/fortune/fortune_archive/1999/06/21/261696/index.htm, May
  10, 2009.
2 Larry Bossidy and Ram Charan, *Execution: The Discipline of Getting Things
  Done* (New York: Crown Business, 2002).
3 Martha Lagace, "What Really Drives Your Strategy? Q&A with: Joseph L.
  Bower and Clark Gilbert," Harvard Business School, January 9, 2006; accessed
  at http://hbswk.hbs.edu/item/5157.html, May 29, 2009.

ACKNOWLEDGMENTS

In writing this book, I have put into practice many of the concepts I present. I have gone from the theory to the practice. Many people talk about writing a book, but doing it takes the right action and dedication every day to make it a reality.

The production of a book goes through many phases, and along the way, I received invaluable advice and inputs to assist me in the final publication.

After the initial manuscript was drafted, industry experts Sheryl Woo, Claire Astle, Shivaramakrishnan Bhaskaran, G. Bala, Michel Sznajer, and Walter Speculand passed me invaluable feedback that helped take the manuscript to another level.

Then the team from John Wiley & Sons in Singapore kicked in and took the manuscript through another refinement before editing and proofreading. Only then did we start on the layout of the book.

I am forever indebted to Suvajit Das from Litt Lindden who worked with Wiley to design the front cover, as he has done for my earlier books.

And—most important—I thank you for purchasing the book.

I

BOARD APPROVAL

After 18 months of discussions and planning, the strategy that will leverage the current market opportunities so as to achieve double-digit growth over the next three years in these turbulent times is locked in. You've met with each of the Board members to gather their feedback on the strategy paper in advance of the crucial meeting, and the time you've spent has paid off. Now you can take a breath, step back, and prepare to implement the strategy, comfortably aware that hardest part is over.

This is the stance adopted by many leaders in many different countries and one that leads in the direction their competition is praying they will take: failure. If you're approaching strategy on this basis, you are at a crossroads where all the signs point in the direction you must not take. The staggering high failure rate on strategy implementation until recently has gone unchecked by leaders around the world. Most strategies, most of the time, accomplish less than half of what their sponsors hoped and planned for.

It's true. Nine out of 10 strategies fail to be implemented successfully.[1]

Implementing strategy is harder than crafting strategy. It doesn't matter if you have the perfect strategy for your circumstances if you don't succeed in implementing it.

Leaders today appreciate that a triumph of implementation can be a Blue Ocean Strategy[2]—that is, a competitive differentiator—and realize that while there are many tools and techniques for crafting a strategy, there are very few for implementing it. Rosabeth Moss Kanter puts it eloquently:

Ethical standards and our ability to groom future leaders inevitably decline. That's why execution, or "making it happen," is so important. Execution is the un-idea; it means having the mental and organizational flexibility to put new business models into practice, even if they counter what you're currently doing. That ability is central to running an organization right now. So rather than chasing another new management fad, or expecting still another "magic bullet" to come along, organizations should focus on execution to effectively use the organizational tools we already have.[3]

To further support Kanter's comment, consider the report from *Barons* that only 15 percent of the 974 programs reviewed in fiscal 2005 were rated effective.

In addition, from 1917 to 1987 only 39 of the original Forbes 100 survived and only two outperformed the market: GE and Eastman Kodak.

It is time to switch the focus from just crafting strategy to *crafting and implementing* it. It is estimated that U.S. managers spend more than $10 billion annually on strategic analysis and strategy formulation. If 90 percent fail, then that is a waste of $9 billion.

Many people think of execution as detail work, that it's below the dignity of business leaders. I think that it's the leader's most important job.
> —Larry Johnston, CEO of Albertsons

Our problem is not about strategy itself but about our execution of it.
> —Tony Howard, CEO of BP, 2007

Implementation is a relatively new field—only about 10 years old—whose genesis is strategy's high failure rate and the lack of a framework to guide leaders. Research on the subject is just being conducted. Bridges Business Consultancy Int. (the organization I founded and run) first published from its research, that 90 percent of strategies fail to be implemented successfully, in 2003. The focus is now to enable leaders by providing them the tools and techniques they need.

What Is Strategy Implementation?

Strategy implementation is collective individual actions taken every day by staff members who will deliver the strategy for tomorrow.

Why Do So Many Strategies Fail to Deliver?

The key word is *action*. Staff members are always busy. The key question is "*Is the work they are doing adding value to the new strategy?*" Are the actions that staff members are taking today driving the implementation forward? We know staff members frequently have more work than they have hours in the day, but implementation is dependent on their taking the right actions.

Many implementations fail because leaders underestimate the implementation challenge and as a result take their eye off what needs to be done. When they do not focus on taking the right actions, neither do their staff members. Another key reason is that they do not have a framework to guide them through the implementation journey.

> One of top management's biggest blind spots is the failure to recognize that any significant shift in strategy requires changes in day-to-day activities throughout the organization. Small shifts may require only minor changes. Significant shifts require significant changes—from subtle to sweeping—that can only be successful if implemented systematically. And people at all levels can either help or hinder the transition.
> —*Morgan, Levitt, and Malek*, Executing Your Strategy

Leaders must stop doing what doesn't work. They must step back and reconsider how they will execute the strategy. This is not a new problem, as the story "Traveling North" shows.

If we keep doing the same thing the way most North Pole—bound sailors did, then no wonder we keep getting our strategy crushed! It is time to change the way we think about implementation. We must go beyond change management as we know it and focus on implementation.

Consider that 30 years ago management was about control and that change management was designed as command and control. However,

Traveling North

In the 1800s, all attempts to reach the North Pole failed. All the ships were designed to push through the ice, but they all—except one—eventually ended up being crushed.

No one could design a ship that could survive the ice, and no one really knew what was at the North Pole: snow ... ice ... land? Since the changing ice kept crushing the ships, most people gave up and thought it impossible.

One of the expeditions that came nearest to success was led by Fridtjof Nansen, who hypothesized that the ice was constantly changing and moving. He said that the ice caps were moving west across the Arctic. His plan was to build a special ship that could rise out of the sea as the ice pressed against her hull, rather than attempt to resist the essentially irresistible forces of pressure and change. He built the *Fram,* which means "Onward" in Norwegian.

After three months of travel, the *Fram* was locked into the ice just north of 78 degrees latitude. As the changing ice converged on the ship, the ship rose out of the water, and for three years, drifted across the ice pack.

Nansen's theory worked—he had conquered the impossible. He had adapted to change and learned to ride with it rather than be crushed by it.

business has dramatically changed. We have moved to empowerment and a teaming approach. Many leaders use change management out of lack of awareness that an alternative approach is available.

Change management methodology is designed for projects and should not be force fitted for strategy implementation.

The Leader's Responsibility in Implementing Strategy

No MBA wants to learn about execution. It's not exciting. Strategy is exciting. The Big Think is exciting. But execution is far more important.
—William Johnson, Chairman and CEO of H.J. Heinz

Leaders have a fundamental responsibility to create the right conditions for implementation in the organization. They must, for example, encourage the right people; clearly communicate the strategy objectives; create the Key Performance Indicators (KPIs); align the culture to the implementation; redesign processes; change the way staff members are reinforced to encourage the right behaviors and actions for the new strategy to be implemented; and then review the strategy implementation every two weeks. This can be an overwhelming list, but if it were easy to deliver the promises of a new strategy, then 90 percent of implementations would not fail. (At Bridges, we regard a new strategy as successful when the leaders deliver at least 50 percent of its goals.)

Leaders must also specifically identify what needs to be done and where to put the organization's focus. Although it is not unheard of for two organizations to have the same strategy—for example, to be number one in the industry or differentiate through customer service or leading product—each organization's implementation of the strategy is unique; leaders, after identifying what needs to be done, must then lead staff members to perform the required behaviors and actions.

After crafting the strategy, leaders must shift from thinking, planning and developing to action, managing resources and strong leadership. Many leaders fail in this transition. For example, translating the strategy into daily actions that staff members must take is tougher than it sounds. On many occasions when working with a leadership team, I discover that the leaders can't explain what they want their people to do differently as a result of hearing about the new strategy. The leadership team understands the strategy, but it has not considered the strategy's implications for the individual areas of the business and its people's day-to-day activities.

One organization I worked with had a strategy to reclaim the number one spot in the country. The strategy had been developed with the assistance of a global consultancy, and the leaders knew what they needed to do. What was not clear was what the staff members were expected to do. We spent time identifying what the strategy meant at the grass roots. On this occasion, it was that everyone at all levels must do things better than the competition, and staff members were given the tools and challenged to improve their own work by 15 percent.

Leaders generally know that implementation requires extra effort. In reality, however, very few are able to free up valuable time and resources to do justice to the implementation journey. They become so caught up in managing the day-to-day business that they lose sight of their goal to implement the new strategy and as such end up taking the wrong actions.

We have a "strategic" plan. It's called doing things.
—Herb Kelleher, ex-CEO of Southwest Airlines

When Do You Stop Planning and Start Implementing?

By the time leaders have completed the strategy and had it printed, circulated and converted into a multimedia presentation, they have probably missed the ideal launch window for the strategy. Many leaders work on the strategy until they think it is finished. This is a mistake.

A strategy is never finished. It only becomes obsolete.

For a strategy to be successful it must be executed. The draft of a strategy is like the architect's plans for a new building, not real until it is built. An effective strategy is created twice, like most things in life—the mental then the physical, the blueprint then the construction, the writing of the music and then the playing of it, the crafting of the strategy and then the implementation.

When leaders implement strategy it never goes according to plan. What the team discussed is never what happens in reality. By the time leaders start rolling out the strategy, markets have changed, customer expectations have shifted, competing products are available, prices have adjusted, and internal conditions have changed. As a result, during the implementation stage, strategy must be adapted and amended. Again, all things are created twice.

The implications of waiting until the strategy is finished and having to take the time to go back upstream means that leaders lose momentum. This can be the death knell of the implementation.

In crafting the strategy, comprehensive market research concerning the market, customers, competition, and financial and internal situation will have been completed. Once the fundamental principles and the outline of the strategy are in place, it is time to start implementing—typically this is about 80 percent of the total strategy crafting. Do not wait to complete the final details and beautify them. Implementation is tough and along the way details change. As soon as you have the core strategy in place, get going.

For more evidence that strategy is perpetually unfinished, consider what happened to British Airways when it opened Heathrow Airport

Terminal Five in April 2008. After 12 months of testing, the baggage system failed. Up to 18,000 bags were lost. Or consider what happened when McDonald's opened its first drive-through in China. Not only was it a first for McDonald's, it was also China's first drive-though. Customers would drive up to the counter and order their meal. They would take it, park their car, and take the meal into the restaurant to sit down at a table!

To successfully implement a strategy, leaders need to review it in parts every two weeks, and the whole strategy every quarter. During the reviews they become aware of what is working and what is not. This is the time to aggressively drive forward and make the strategy come alive. Leaders drive the organization forward on both the plan and the execution. They do not base decisions on just theory, but on theory, actions, and reactions. This provides a strong springboard to successfully move the implementation forward.

Don't hesitate, start going. Don't analyze too long. If there is a mistake in the thinking, it will be identified in the regular reviews to ensure everything is going to plan. If not, then you correct what is not working.

No one starts out with a strategy known to be bad. It is only when you start implementing that its quality (or lack of quality) becomes apparent. It is only if you're constantly reviewing the strategy implementation that you will know what is working and what is not.

The Implementation Plan

Execution is so important for a company—while good strategy certainly helps, it is on the basis of execution that you generally succeed or fail.
—Andrew Penn, CEO of AXA, Australia

While working with different clients, one constant I see is a poor implementation plan. I do see excellent launches and excellent communication plans, but very few good implementation plans. The difference is that an implementation plan needs to be based on an organization's current strengths and weaknesses as they affect its ability to execute the strategy and identify the right actions to be taken in the short term for long-term performance. It is not about a town hall meeting, posters on the walls, or coffee mugs with a logo.

The crafting of the implementation plan should be part of the crafting of the strategy agenda. The same people who are involved in the strategy crafting should be involved in crafting and overseeing its implementation.

Far too often, implementation is delegated. Leaders feel that after they have crafted their strategy, they can move on, sure that most of their work is complete. But this is not the case. Most implementations fail, and two contributing factors to this are the failure to develop a comprehensive implementation plan and the failure of leaders to take personal responsibility. This means spending twice as much effort and time to implement the strategy as to create it.

In a nutshell—strategy is the "big think," and implementation is taking the right action.

Lee Hsien Loong, Singapore's prime minister, is quoted as saying:

An unpolished plan vigorously executed is more successful than an ideal plan implemented with less determination. Better to strike energetically, gain experience, learn what works and what does not, reassess the new situation, devise fresh plans and take another step. Spend too long preparing elaborate plans, and you will lose both time and initiative.

In developing a high-quality implementation, plan leaders must analyze their organization's readiness for implementation and use a framework to ensure they're taking the right actions. Both of these are essential differences to current implementation thinking. Most leaders assume that once you have crafted the strategy, the organization is ready to implement it and that staff members will automatically take the right actions. Chapter 2 outlines how you can conduct the analysis and identify the right actions to successfully implement the strategy.

He who every morning plans the transaction of the day and follows out that plan carries a thread that will guide them through the maze of the most busy life. But where no plan is laid, where the disposal of time is surrendered merely to the chance of incidence, chaos will soon reign.

—Victor Hugo

Napoleon allegedly said that no successful battle ever followed its plan. Yet Napoleon also planned every one of his battles far more meticulously than any earlier general had done. Without an action plan, the executive becomes a prisoner of events.

Deliver the Promise

Leaders are paid for creating shareholder return. The question is, "How will they deliver their promise to the shareholder?" In the annual shareholders meeting, the plans are outlined and the leadership have responsibility to deliver on the promise.

Only with both a strong strategy and strong implementation will leaders deliver the results as the diagram in Figure 1.1 explains.

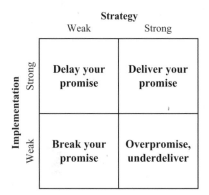

Figure 1.1   Impact of implementation.

The implications of the four quadrants break out as follows:

Break your promise	You have made a promise to the shareholders, Board, customers, and staff members, and do not deliver on it. This is criminal.
Overpromise, underdeliver	This is what the majority of leaders are guilty of doing. It is unforgivable.
Delay your promise	You have made the promise and may well keep it, but it takes you longer to get there. This is unacceptable.
Deliver your promise	You have made the promise and you deliver it on schedule. This is rare, but the payoff is tremendous.

If you would like a summary of the Bridges research, please send an e-mail to bridges@bridgesconsultancy.com with the subject "research summary."

Summary—Leaders' Role in Implementation

Five things leaders must do differently:

1. **Focus on both crafting and implementing strategy.**
   Implementing strategy is harder than creating it. Of every 10 strategies, 9 fail to be implemented successfully. Research by Bridges and others supports this. The challenge for leaders is to take the effort and time they spend crafting the strategy and at least double both when they craft the implementation, and to translate the strategy into daily actions for the staff members.
   Strategy implementation is the collective individual actions taken every minute of every day by every staff member. Without enough of the right actions being taken, the strategy is heading for the graveyard.

2. **Create the right conditions.**
   Leaders have a fundamental responsibility to create the right conditions in their organizations. They must, for example, encourage the right people; clearly communicate the strategy objectives; create KPIs; align the culture to the implementation; redesign processes; change the way staff members are reinforced to encourage the right behaviors and actions for the new strategy to be implemented; and review the strategy implementation every two weeks. This can be an overwhelming list, but if it were easy to deliver all the promises of a new strategy, then 9 out of 10 implementations would not fail.

3. **Identify what needs to be done.**
   Leaders must identify what needs to be done and where to put the organization's focus. Although it is not unheard of for two organizations to have the same strategy—for example, number one in the industry or differentiate through customer service or leading products—each organization's implementation of the strategy is unique and leaders must identify what needs to be done under the specific conditions their organization faces.

They must lead staff members to perform the required behaviors and actions.

This requires a shift in leadership mind-set and focus. There must be a new realization that crafting strategy is only the first chapter in the book of success and that implementation takes considerably more time and effort than most leaders anticipate. Leaders must stay focused on the implementation and make sure that staff members are taking the right actions.

4. **Adapt and amend the strategy.**
   Implementation never goes according to plan. Customer expectations shift, markets move, products change, and employee turnover fluctuates; these are just some of the factors that mean what is planned in the boardroom is not what happens in the implementation.

   Once leaders implement a strategy they need to review it in parts every two weeks, and the whole strategy every quarter. During the reviews, they become aware of what is working and what is not. This is the time to aggressively drive forward and make the strategy come alive. Leaders drive the organization forward on both the plan and the execution. They do not base their decisions on theory alone, but on theory, actions, and reactions.

5. **Create an implementation plan.**
   In developing a high-quality implementation plan, leaders must analyze their organization's readiness for implementation and use a framework to ensure they're taking the right actions. Both of these are essential differences to current implementation thinking. Most leaders assume that once you have crafted the strategy, the organization is ready to implement it and staff members will automatically take the right actions—but history shows that they are wrong.

Endnotes

1 Based on eight years of research by Bridges Business Consultancy Int.
2 W. C. Kim and R. Mauborgne, *Blue Ocean Strategy: How to Create Uncontested Market Space and Make Competition Irrelevant* (Boston: Harvard Business Publishing, 2005).
3 R. M. Kanter, "Execution: The Un-Idea," *Strategy+Business*, December 12, 2005; Accessed at www.strategy-business.com/press/enewsarticle/enews121205?pg=0, May 31, 2009.

4 I. Cobbold and G. Lawrie, "Why do only one third of UK companies realise significant strategic success?" 2GC Working Paper, 2GC Limited, May 2001.
5 P. Kotter, *Leading Change* (Cambridge: Harvard Business School Press, 1996).
6 M. C. Mankins and R. Steele, "Turning Great Strategy into Great Performance," *Harvard Business Review,* July-August 2005; accessed at www.bestyearyet.com/Teams/Turning-Great-Strategy.pdf, June 1, 2009.

2

A FRAMEWORK FOR IMPLEMENTING STRATEGY

Despite the growth of research and the number of books and articles on implementation that have appeared over the last few years, leaders still have a very limited choice of frameworks to address the challenge of implementing strategy.

Probably the best-known framework is the Balanced Scorecard from Kaplan and Norton. Developed in the early 1990s, it has revolutionized the way organizations measure performance, and it provided a management system for running the businesses. The framework emphasizes that you need to do more than measure the lag indicators of finance—you need to also track measures of customer response, internal processes, and learning and growth. The authors also created a one-page summary of an organization's strategy, a "Strategy Map," based on a five-step framework:

- Mobilize change through executive leadership.
- Translate strategy to operational terms.
- Align the organization to strategy.
- Motivate to make strategy everybody's job.
- Govern to make strategy a continuing process.

This book builds on the Implementation Compass™, a framework I developed several years ago to guide organizations in implementation by identifying the right actions. The eight points of the compass, shown in Figure 2.1, represent eight key elements that need constant attention if the effort is to succeed. The eight elements or directions of the compass—People, Biz Case, Communicate, Measure, Culture, Process, Reinforce, and Review—provide chapter headings for the body of this book

Advantages of the Implementation Compass:

1. Works for both small and large organizations.
2. Allows you to assess your current status in preparing to implement your strategy.
3. Guides you through the eight critical directions.
4. Provides a basis for your implementation plan.
5. Identifies the *right* action.
6. Keeps implementation on the leadership radar.

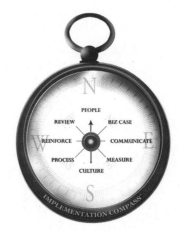

Figure 2.1   The Implementation Compass.

Many leaders return to their office after launching a new strategy with no plan of action on how to identify what to do next and instruct their people accordingly. They need to do a variety of things:

- Figure out how to inform the people in their division of the imminent changes.
- Explain what needs to change and why.
- Review the way the team is working.
- Ensure that the current rewards and recognition systems support the new strategy.
- Motivate their people.
- Assess the current measures being used.

This multitude of activities creates a maze in which it is easy to get lost. Many leaders delegate the implementation and take their eyes off what needs to be done. This leads to failure. The Implementation Compass helps leaders identify how they can translate their strategy into actions for staff members, and specify what needs to be done first.

Let's be honest: being invited by a CEO to help create an organization's future strategy is perceived as flattering, an opportunity to prove oneself that could lead to promotion. Being invited by a CEO to help implement the strategy is often perceived as laborious and even a punishment—even though it is not strategy that creates revenue but its implementation.

Victory is much more meaningful when it comes not just from the efforts of one person but from the joint achievements of many.

The euphoria is lasting when all participants lead with their hearts, winning not just for themselves but for one another.

Success is sweet when it is shared.

—John Scully, Former Chairman of Apple Computers

Leaders Need to Be Cognizant of Their Implementation Responsibilities

Successful implementation, though not rocket science, does take discipline and structure. It is about doing many right things all at once. As you implement strategy, you move from theory to practice, from planning to action, and from concept to execution. The critical question becomes, "What are the actions you need to take?"

This may sound like a simple question, but in practice it is the driver of successful implementation, because successful implementation is all about identifying the right actions to take and then ensuring they are done to create the right results. The 1999 *Fortune* article, "Why CEOs Fail," asserted that the best practice among the best CEOs is their follow-up.[1] At the start of every meeting, they checked that actions were taken from the last meeting and that the right outcomes were achieved. It is the actions that you take every day in your business that either move you closer to your strategy or further away.

At Bridges, we surveyed businesses from various industries over an eight-year period about the challenges they face when implementing strategy. The results are as follows:

Ranking	Challenge
1	Ensuring staff members take different actions or demonstrate different behaviors
2	Communicating change
3	Gaining support among the people in the organization
4	Tracking success of implementation with a measurement tool
5	Gaining support of senior management
6	Changing rewards and recognition
7	Implementing new technology
8	Aligning processes
9	Acquiring customer feedback

Implementation is a business differentiator. It is a key difference between success and failure, and can no longer be ignored. By excelling in implementation, you can create outstanding results.

Eight Directions, Equal Importance

On the Implementation Compass, all eight directions are important, but their individual degree of importance varies for each organization.

A client we worked with in the telecom industry initiated the implementation of its strategy by first focusing on the measures. It then started to redesign the processes to support the strategy, and then moved to working with staff to ensure decisions being made were based on the strategic objectives and not the operational objectives.

We recently met with a manufacturing CEO for the first time, and we presented the Implementation Compass. He told us that two years earlier, he had launched a strategic initiative that had failed, making him realize that he had to do something different. He immediately pointed to Communicate and Culture on the compass and identified these two as the weakest elements. Focusing on these two elements, while still including the others, we were able to support the CEO in a successful implementation.

The Implementation Compass also helps organizations to maintain momentum throughout the journey. Strategy implementation has a habit of losing momentum. It is just not the exciting part of the strategy. It typically takes twice as long, involves managing the details, and conflicts with many other day-to-day challenges. As a result, implementation gets lost in the burden of running the business. By simultaneously addressing each of the eight directions, leadership can stay focused on what still needs to be done.

The Implementation Compass also allows leaders to perform an assessment of the organization's readiness to implement the strategy and the organization's strengths and weaknesses with respect to the strategy implementation.

Strategy Implementation Readiness Assessment

After crafting the strategy, where do you begin on the implementation journey?

One of the first steps to ensure that strategy is successfully implemented is to assess how ready your organization is to implement the strategy. The Strategy Implementation Readiness Assessment is a tool based on the eight directions. It provides key questions for leaders and staff members that will help them identify their organization's strengths and weaknesses with reference to its readiness to implement the new strategy.

Change initiatives often fail because leaders don't reconcile or even understand their internal capabilities and the complexity of their external worlds.
    —Adjunct Professor Michael Jarret, London Business School

Leaders in transition reflexively rely on the skills and strategies that worked for them in the past, but those approaches won't necessarily work in new environments. To move seamlessly into new roles, executives need an accurate read of the business situation at hand—for instance, are they moving into a turnaround or a simple realignment of operations? Strong leadership right out of the gate, plus a common language for change that can accelerate everyone's transition into new roles and opportunities.
    —Michael Watkins, co-founder of Genesis Advisers

Bridges conducts Strategy Implementation Readiness Assessments for clients so that they can understand their internal capabilities. The process involves one-on-one interviews with leaders and interviews with staff members in groups of 10 to 12 over two days. After completing all the research, a radar diagram is drawn to visually reflect the organizational Strategy Implementation Readiness Assessment.

Here are some samples of the questions asked around the eight directions:

- *People.* It is not leadership that implements strategy but people.

  Do you have the right caliber of people?

  Do they have the skills and knowledge to execute the new strategy?

  Are they motivated to do so?

- *Biz Case.* You need an emotional and numerical rationale for adopting the strategy.

  Do all your staff members know what the new strategy is?

  Do your staff members know why it is important?

  How motivated are they to participate in the implementation?

- *Communicate.* People can only adopt a strategy if they know and understand it.

  Can the leaders explain the objectives of the new strategy so as to obtain buy-in?

  Do staff members know the new actions and behaviors they must take to implement it?

  Are there regular ongoing communications about success, best practices, lessons and learned throughout the implementation?

- *Measure.* You must have the right measures in place to drive the right behaviors and actions.

  How well have new corporate wide measures been identified to track the success of the new strategy?

  How well are leaders adopting new measures in the regular management meetings?

  Do the measures drive the right behaviors and actions?

- *Culture.* You must change the day-to-day activities of your staff members and have a culture that supports and fosters change.

  How well does the current culture support the new strategy?

How prepared is the organization to adopt the new strategy?

Has leadership changed the fundamental way the organization works so as to encourage the adoption of the new strategy, for example, meetings, leadership style, discussion?

- *Process.* There must be congruence between what you say you are going to do (strategy implementation) and what you are doing (the process).

Do your processes support the new strategy?

How ready are you to redesign your processes?

How well do you know which processes you need redesigned?

- *Reinforce.* You must reinforce the expected actions and behaviors so that they are continuously repeated.

When staff members step into the unknown and demonstrate the new actions and behaviors, are they recognized and rewarded?

Does the reinforcement encourage them to continue to demonstrate the desired new actions and behaviors?

How well are leaders supporting and encouraging staff performers by being visible, walking around, and leading by example?

- *Review* The weakest of the eight points among leaders—you must constantly review to make sure the right actions and behaviors are being taken to deliver the right results.

Are the actions and behaviors being taken producing the right results?

Do you know what lessons have been learned from the implementation in the last 90 days?

Do you know what you need to start doing differently from today?

Once the assessment is complete, the findings are reflected as a radar diagram, as shown in Figure 2.2.

A quick look at the figure reveals two major areas of concern. Actions need to be discussed for communication of the strategy to the whole organization, and for redesign of the processes to support the strategy.

Just as important, the figure identifies strengths in the areas of people and measures are identified. It is imperative to continue to

Figure 2.2 Strategy Implementation Readiness Assessment Radar.

work on the organization's strengths as well as its weaknesses. Too often leaders take their focus off what is successful and concentrate on the weaknesses, and as a result the strengths start to deteriorate

As Peter Drucker used to say:

Whenever one makes a key decision and whenever one does a key action, one writes down what one expects will happen. And nine months or 12 months later, one then feeds back from results to expectations. I have been doing this for some 15 to 20 years now. And every time I do it, I am surprised. And so is everyone who has ever done this.

Within a fairly short period of time, maybe two or three years, this simple procedure will tell people first where their strengths are—and this is probably the most important thing to know about oneself. It will show them what they do or fail to do that deprives them of the full yield from their strengths. It will show them where they are not particularly competent. And finally, it will show them where *they* have no strengths and cannot perform.

After the strengths and weaknesses have been identified, the next step is to identify what actions need to be taken to drive the implementation. At Bridges, we start off by asking five simple-seeming questions that do a great deal to help identify the right actions:

What should we...

Question	Example
Do more of	Currently we conduct annual customer research, but to be customer-centric, we need to conduct research every quarter.
Do less of	We are currently holding too many internal meetings that distract staff members from taking the actions we need them to take.
Keep doing	Feedback has been very positive on the monthly strategy update from each staff member's immediate boss and we will continue this.
Start doing	We will create a recognition program to support the new behaviors.
Stop doing	We will no longer form committees; instead we will make individual people responsible.

Stop Doing

Though this item is last on the list of questions, it may be the most important going forward. Almost all leaders have a to-do list, but how many have a "to-stop" list? In implementation, you need a to-stop list. If you are changing your strategy, then you are asking your organization to do something different and it is critical to identify the old behaviors and actions that no longer add value under the new strategy. When we work with a leadership team on the strategy implementation, the to-stop list tends to be twice as long as the to-do list. This immediately clarifies to staff members what they should stop and start doing, and it reinforces what is important and what is not relevant to the new strategy.

Each time an organization changes, it must go from equilibrium to chaos and back to equilibrium. During the initial transformation, there is always confusion among staff members on what they should focus on. The to-stop list in conjunction with the to-do list goes a long way toward rectifying the confusion. Staff members also appreciate that they are not just being asked to do more work and that the leadership has taken the time to identify what is no longer relevant to the business.

Strategic Project Review

On completion of the Strategy Implementation Readiness Assessment and before you start implementing the strategy, a review of the different strategic projects running across the organization should be conducted to check their alignment with the new strategy. This is an onerous exercise for many organizations, as it is when the rubber hits the road with respect to implementing the strategy. It is often the first time leaders are asked to put the theory into practice and make decisions that impact current business plans. It is decision time.

While we were working with one client, the CEO arranged a one-day offsite for his team to review current strategic projects and to discuss the implementation plan. Although during the day the leaders participating agreed with the CEO, their actions afterward were not as compliant. Many of them dragged their feet and held on to current projects even though the team had agreed they were no longer of value! At the second review, one month later, the CEO had to switch his style from democratic to autocratic and come down hard on leaders who had not ended projects as agreed. This created the right response in that the team saw the commitment and sincerity of the CEO to the new strategy. It was a battle worth fighting as it also went on to set the tone for the two-weekly reviews.

A current best practice in many organizations is to set up a strategic project office or office of strategy management that works like an internal consulting group. Its job is to conduct the strategic project review and also take on these essential tasks:

- Coordinate projects across the organization.
- Ensure projects stay on schedule.
- Share best practices.
- Provide skills and expertise when required.
- Communicate the corporate strategy.
- Keep the CEO informed of progress.

The strategic project office or office of strategy management is not responsible for doing the implementation but for overseeing it. Everyone is responsible for strategy implementation and the responsibility can't be delegated to one department.

This office, or a specifically selected team from the leadership, identifies and then reviews current projects and decides whether to continue, amend, or stop each project depending on the value it contributes to the new strategy. With limited resources in any organization, a strong focus can go a long way to ensuring success.

Funding Implementation

The funding of implementation does not come from the organization's annual budget. On the occasions we have observed attempts to cover it with regularly budgeted funds, the implementation typically fizzled out, as there was no investment in the organization's future. Leaders must put the money where they want to see action.

The implementation plan must have independent funding from the budget. If you falter at this stage because the CEO or the Board will not provide this funding, you have a very clear indicator that the implementation will fail; they are not truly committed to it.

If there is an office of strategy management or director of strategy, then that is who is responsible for the funding with a direct line to the CEO. (Meaning the chief *execution* officer!)

The next eight chapters discuss in detail the leaders' role in each of the eight global best practices that form the Implementation Compass.

Summary—Leaders' Role in Implementation

Four things leaders must do differently:

1. **Identify the right framework.**
   Leaders are responsible for identifying a framework to guide the organization through the implementation maze. Without a framework, the chances of achieving the strategic objectives and goals are dramatically reduced. Also, many organizations are taking action, but not the actions that are driving the implementation forward.

   One framework to consider adopting is the Implementation Compass, which assists leaders in identifying how they can translate the strategy into actions for their staff members and identifies what needs to be done first.

2. **Conduct a strategy implementation readiness assessment.**
   A novel approach to assist implementation is to assess how ready the organization is to implement the strategy, rather than just assuming that once the strategy has been crafted, it will be adopted.

   Leaders step back from the day-to-day business and take the time to assess the strengths and weaknesses of the organization against the eight global best practices of implementation. They then identify the specific actions that will drive the implementation forward, as it is the actions that are taken every day that move you either closer to your strategy or further away.

As well as identifying what to start doing, leaders must also identify what should be stopped. A new strategy not only means doing things differently, it also means leaders must identify what staff members should stop doing that no longer adds value.

Every implementation is unique and the assessment will ensure that leaders do not just come up with a generic plan, but one that is specific to the culture, needs, and requirements of the organization. It will also ensures that leaders are preparing the organization for success by identifying the right actions to take today to make the strategy come alive tomorrow.

3. **Review current projects for alignment.**
   A current best practice in many organizations is to set up a strategic project office or office for strategic management to review current projects in the organization. Projects are continued, amended, or stopped, depending on the value they contribute to the new strategy. With limited resources in any organization, a strong focus can go a long way to ensuring success.

4. **Fund the implementation.**
   Leaders must put the money where they want to see action and ensure that, if required, there is funding for the implementation, separate from the annual budget.

Endnote

1 Ram Charan and Geoffrey Colvin, "Why CEOs Fail: It's rarely for lack of smarts or vision. Most unsuccessful CEOs stumble because of one simple, fatal shortcoming," *Fortune*, June 21, 1999, p. 68; accessed at http://money. cnn.com/magazines/fortune/fortune_archive/1999/06/21/261696/index.htm, May 10, 2009.

3

PEOPLE

Your most precious possession is not your financial assets. Your most precious possession is the people you have working there and what they carry around in their heads and their ability to work together.
  —Robert Reich, American economist and politician

Change doesn't come from a slogan or a speech. It happens because you put the right people in place to make it happen.
  —Jack Welch

At North on the compass—People, the ones who implement strategy. The objective of this chapter is to identify how leaders can engage staff members, encourage them to take the right actions, and perform the right behaviors. The people are leaders' strategy customers.

Also in this chapter, I address the mistaken belief that most people resist implementation, and look at why leaders cannot delegate implementation.

Strategy Customers

When implementing strategy, you are selling it to the staff members and they are the ones who must buy it (buy-in). This is a paradigm shift for many leaders. In most implementations, leaders delegate the responsibility to their staff members without proper support, encouragement, and the appropriate tools and techniques. Leaders then sit back and expect the implementation to be carried out effectively

Leaders need to adopt the same mind-set for rolling out a strategy to the organization as they would adopt, for example, in launching a new product to customers. When leaders take the time to show staff members respect, staff members take the time to do the same.

Take the time to sit down with your team and discuss the new strategy. Consider asking them:

- How does the strategy impact your work?
- How does the strategy impact your department?
- How does the strategy impact you personally?
- What concerns do you have about the new strategy?
- What needs to change for you to successfully adopt the strategy?
- What new skills do you feel you need to execute the strategy?
- What can I do to support you while you implement the strategy?
- What will you do differently in your everyday work?

If you work with your staff members during implementation in the same way you work with customers when launching a product, you improve the way you view your people, and as a result your, staff members will more readily adopt the strategy and resist it less.

People Do Not Resist Change

When the leadership announces a change in strategic direction, what is the typical reaction? Most believe that people will resist most of the time. My research reveals otherwise. This is probably one of the most controversial arguments in the book, and it is certainly the one where I see the most doubtful faces in the audience when I present it. But keep in mind that if 90 percent of implementations are failing to deliver, there must be something wrong in the current approach and thinking.

For years, we have churned along with the notion that when organizations are making large changes, most people resist. This assumed resistance, we figured, could be from a fear of losing responsibility or stepping into the unknown, or of trying new things, and so we have crafted strategy implementation and people policies based on these assumptions.

By contrast, eight years of Bridges research has established that when it comes to implementation in an organization, most people do not resist it—if the new strategy is presented and communicated correctly.

The Four Groups

The launch of a new strategy means that leaders are asking staff members to do things differently. They must change the way they do their everyday work. Most staff members will do this if they understand the reason for the change, and see that it is not just change for the sake of change.

You will get some resistance. In a typical organization, 20 percent (and only 20 percent) resist change. These people tend to complain about anything and everything. They badmouth the implementation behind the leader's back and complain that the money could be spent better on bonuses instead of a lost cause like this. They believe and convince others around them that this is yet another management fad. Based on these characteristics, we at Bridges call such people *saboteurs*. If they win, the whole implementation fails.

The bulk of the staff—the middle 60 percent—fence-sitters. These people neither support the implementation nor oppose it. They come into work at 9 AM and leave at 6 PM. In between, they simply do their jobs. They don't volunteer for additional work, but they don't actively resist change either. Based on their characteristics, we call them *groupies*. Groupies like safety in numbers.

The final 20 percent are those who welcome the change, embrace it and willingly support it. They are the early adopters and are drivers of the change. Based on their characteristics, we call them *mavericks*.

There is one more group who are not easy to see as they are hidden among the saboteurs. Based on their characteristics, we call them *double agents.* They initially resist, but can become mavericks. Double agents have seen change many times before and are doubtful it will succeed. Double agents wait until they are sure the organization is serious about the change before committing, but when they do commit, they can become your loudest and strongest mavericks.

So why is there the notion that people resist change?

Of all the groups, saboteurs make the most noise and as a result they create the largest impression. This leads people to the wrong perception that most people resist change. The reality, however, is that the only group that steadfastly resists change is this small minority called saboteurs.

Professor Edward Lawler of the University of Southern California argues that people are not born with a gene to automatically resist change. He says, "People's reaction to the change depends on their experience, how it is presented and the nature of the change."

Most staff members will go along with the new strategy if you take the time to present and communicate why the new strategy is important and what it will mean to them. This is discussed in detail in the next two chapters.

How to identify these groups in your organization and their mottos? Watch out for these following typical traits:

Groupies

Groupies avoid the spotlight and the center of attention, and they tend to be passive, even when the change is an opportunity for them. Being a groupie is not bad; these people are the backbone of your organization. They do the day-to-day work that has to be done. To them, work is just work and they often have greater interests outside, such as being a member of a sports team.

Groupies' motto: "Safety in numbers"

Saboteurs

Saboteurs are out to block the implementation. If they win, you lose. To identify saboteurs in your organization ask, "Who is likely to respond actively, but see the change as a threat?" These people will make a lot of noise and take a lot of actions, but the wrong actions!

Saboteurs' motto: "Status quo"

Double Agents

Initially, double agents appear to oppose the implementation. They stand back to see if this strategy is just another management fad, or if it will last. When they see that it is succeeding, however, they switch from opposing it to being strong supporters. Only by their own free will can double agents cross over and become supporters. This happens once they see the desired actions taking place. To identify double agents in your organization ask, "Who is likely to respond actively and see the change as a threat, but is open to persuasion?" Double agents can be convinced only through actions, not words.

> *Double agents' motto:* "After all is said and done, more is said than done"

Mavericks

Mavericks willingly and enthusiastically support the implementation. To identify mavericks in your organization ask, "Who is likely to respond actively to the force of change and see it as an opportunity?" In most organizations, leaders do not recognize and reward mavericks enough.

> *Mavericks' motto:* "It is easier to ask for forgiveness than permission"

Research from Associate Professor Boris Groysberg at Harvard Business School reveals that the top 1 percent of staff members tend to outperform average workers by 127 percent!

Focus on Mavericks

By focusing on mavericks, the organization generates critical traction from early wins that can also be shared and celebrated with the rest of the organization. In addition, mavericks provide leaders with the necessary feedback for tweaking and improving the implementation. While this positive group is adopting the implementation, it influences the middle group. Remember, those in the middle group sit on the fence and could fall either way. If they are influenced by the positive 20 percent, they will start to respond positively to the implementation.

They are the followers. Although that middle 60 percent do not have the enthusiasm and drive to charge out of the starting gate, you can move them along at a steady pace and in the right direction.

Many leaders are drawn to the saboteurs, attempting to find ways to turn them into supporters, as it is human nature to try and please everyone. This is a recipe for failure as saboteurs are like a black hole. They consume all your energy.

The right group to focus on is the 20 percent who welcome and support the new strategy—the mavericks. This is because implementing strategy is difficult. The odds are stacked against you before you even start. We need to make it as easy as possible for the organization to succeed. The 20 percent who support the implementation come on board more readily than the others. Many of them recognize the need for change without being told the reasons. They see the benefits and immediately start to take action.

When we focus our energy on the mavericks and groupies, you create very different people implementation strategies.

Once you have 80 percent of the organization moving in the right direction, you have created a critical mass and built up enough impetus for the strategy to start. But what happens to the remaining 20 percent, who resist the change? About half of these (10 percent of the total staff) will resist but, if handled correctly, will eventually start to move in the right direction. They drag their feet and make a lot of noise. Ultimately, they fall into line. The remaining 10 percent, if you are lucky, will leave your organization and join your favorite competitor! Maybe they had the right competencies when they were hired, but today they will slow you down and possibly cause trouble. Regard them as not being right for the job. It is time to say, "Thank you and good-bye!"

General Electric uses a similar approach called the "Vitality Curve," which is the shape of a bell curve. It identifies the top 20 percent of performers, the middle 70 percent, and the bottom 10 percent.[1]

In Applebee's casual dining segment of the restaurant business, where they have high turnover, they measure the staff turnover of the top 20 percent of performers in each restaurant, the middle 60 percent, and the bottom 20 percent. Managers are rewarded for their success in retaining the top 80 percent, and they are not penalized when the bottom 20 percent leave the company.[2]

Cisco CEO John Chambers identified that 20 percent of his leadership team had to leave the organization when it could not make the transition to a collaborative model. He also changed compensation from individualistic to collaborative, and forced people to work with others.[3]

New Strategy, New Skills

The launch of a new strategy means that you are asking staff members to do things differently. It is the leaders' responsibility to identify any new skills, knowledge, or attitudes that staff members may need and to provide specific training.

The emphasis is placed on specific training. In many failed implementations, a common pattern was that the organization addressed the issue of training by running a generic organization-wide program. Unfortunately, this is all it did, and after the training, staff members returned to their jobs to find that nothing around them changed. Some started to practice the new training, but as they received little or no encouragement, they soon returned to doing things the way they had always done them.

Leaders need to both identify specific training required and reinforce the training once it has been delivered.

Neither of these practices is rocket science, but it is beyond belief how much money organizations spend on training without following up. Competency models assist in identifying the specific training each person needs to execute the strategy. In addition, once an organization provides the right training, it must ensure that staff members are encouraged at every step to put into practice the new skills, knowledge, or attitude they have learned. The environment around the staff members must change as well.

Their immediate boss must recognize and encourage them when they demonstrate the new behaviors or actions, and there must be alignment in the organization's rewards and recognition.

In Chapter 9, I will discuss in detail how to use competency training and ensure that staff members are reinforced to execute the new strategy.

Summary—Leaders' Role in Implementation

Four things leaders must do differently:

1. **Consider staff members as strategy customers.**
   Leaders sell the strategy to staff members and they are the ones who must buy into it. This is a paradigm shift for many leaders. In most implementations, leaders delegate the responsibility to

their staff members without proper support, encouragement, and the appropriate tools and techniques. Leaders then sit back and expect the implementation to be carried out effectively!

The leaders' role is to engage staff members so that they become engaged in the implementation.

2. **Recognize that staff members do not automatically resist change.**
   If 9 out of 10 implementations are failing, there must be something wrong in the current approach and thinking. Most staff members will go along with a new strategy if leaders take the time to present and communicate why the new strategy is important, what it will mean to them, and what they should do to participate in its roll-out.

   Twenty percent strongly support you—the mavericks. Sixty percent will go with the flow—the groupies. Twenty percent will resist—the saboteurs. Among the saboteurs is a small group who have seen it all before and will eventually participate, but only when they see enough implementation traction—the double agents.

3. **Focus on the mavericks.**
   By focusing on mavericks—the 20 percent at the forefront of adopting the new policy—the organization generates traction from early wins that can be shared and celebrated with the rest of the organization. Remember, the odds are stacked against you before you even start.

   In addition, mavericks provide leaders with the feedback necessary for tweaking and improving the implementation. While this positive group is adopting the implementation, it influences the middle group—the groupies—and this will start to create critical mass.

   Many leaders are drawn to focus on the saboteurs, as it is human nature to try and please everyone. This is a recipe for failure as saboteurs are like a black hole. They consume all your energy.

4. **Identify new skills, knowledge, or attitudes that staff members need**
   Leaders must not just roll out a single organization-wide training program. It is essential to identify any specific skills, knowledge, and attitude training that staff members need to be able to successfully execute the strategy.

Endnotes

1 John Welch Jr. "The Vitality Curve," September 2005; accessed at www.eep2.com/images/chalk/0905/020905.htm, June 11, 2009.
2 Aaron Dalton, "Applebee's Turnover Recipe, May 2005; accessed at www.workforce.com/archive/article/24/05/60.php, June 11, 2009.
3 Bronwyn Fryer and Thomas A. Stewart, "Cisco Sees the Future: An Interview with John Chambers," *Harvard Business Review*, November 2008, pp. 72–79.

4

BIZ CASE

There are two ways to persuade people. The first is by using conventional rhetoric, which is what most executives are trained in. That's not good enough, because people are not inspired to act by reason alone. The other way to persuade people—and ultimately a much more powerful way—is by uniting an idea with an emotion. The best way to do that is by telling a compelling story.

—Bronwyn Fryer, Senior Editor at *Harvard Business Review*

To spark an epidemic, ideas must be memorable and move us to action.

—Malcolm Gladwell, *Tipping Point*

In this chapter, I discuss the importance of the Biz Case, how it must explain the importance of the new strategy to the survival of the organization and why it must create a sense of urgency. The Biz Case is critical to the successful execution of your strategy.

Strategy cannot be implemented if it cannot be understood, and it cannot be understood if it cannot be explained.

This means that spelling out the Biz Case is an essential step. When leaders fail to present the Biz Case, the adoption rate of the new strategy is dramatically slower, organization-wide rejection of the strategy becomes likely, and staff members rarely change the way they are working. The story "But Where Will the Days Go?" dramatizes the effect of failing to explain the Biz Case.

But Where Will the Days Go?

Most nations of Europe adopted the Gregorian calendar (the system predominantly in use today) in the 18th century, but Russia only decided to do so after the October revolution in 1917. The official decision to change caused consternation in the minds of the Russian peasants. They believed that they were being robbed of several days of life, because of adjustments to the date. The ensuing riots saw hundreds of innocent, enraged people killed. Change was simply inconceivable.

When the Biz Case is presented to the staff members in the right format, it explains why the new strategy must be adopted and will start to convince the unconvinced.

The key word in the above sentence is *format*. When leaders present the strategy to the Board, it is naturally a more left-brain argument supported by projections, graphs, and a strategy paper. When taking the strategy to the whole organization, a more right-brain argument must be presented. The Biz Case should capture both the mind and the heart, just as a brand captures the minds and hearts of its customers.

Branding the Strategy: The Emotional and Numerical Story

The goal of the Biz Case is to present the strategy in a format that is easy to understand and that encourages staff members to become engaged in its execution. To achieve this, the strategy is given a brand that captures its essence in images and memorable taglines—just like external branding for a consumer product. One image still speaks a thousand words.

No matter how complicated the strategy, leaders must find a way to make it easy to be understood by the whole organization. This challenge is habitually underestimated.

Staff members must know why the new strategy is important. By the time leaders are ready to launch the strategy, they have been living and breathing it for at least six months and understand not only why it is important but what needs to be done. In many organizations, they forget that staff members are seeing the new strategy for the first time and still need to go through the same emotional experience that they have just been through to understand why it is important.

The leadership team must explain the strategy's implications to every staff member, as every staff member must understand the strategy before they can deliver it.

Branding the strategy involves identifying its key messages: the two to four points that underpin the new strategy and establish its importance. These messages need to be identified and translated into clear, self-explanatory images to help bring the strategy to life.

With one client, the organization was changing the company-wide operating platform as part of a strategy to focus on front-end activities related to its business, to support growth, and to broaden its Internet strategy to better support their clients. The new operating platform was a convergence of several existing and new systems. The leader of the convergence took the time to explain the Biz Case. A theme of space was identified as the branding, and it played on the message of launching a new platform and taking a step forward. Messages included

- Destination Within Sight—you'll soon be embarking on a new adventure.
- No Turning Back Now—you've made it halfway to another world.
- Mission Accomplished, Welcome to the New Frontier—Congratulations. You have made the journey of convergence. Take a deep breath and a leap forward.

At the same time, small launch briefings were conducted and time was taken to explain to the staff members:

- The rationale for a new operating platform
- What the new operating platform is
- How it will affect customers
- How it will affect us
- What is not affected
- How we can help you in this transition
- Project milestones
- How we are organized to deliver this new operating platform
- What the next steps will be

The transition to the new platform had numerous challenges—not least, ensuring that the transition was seamless to customers. The time taken by the leaders to work on the Biz Case helped staff members understand what was wrong with the old operating system and why they had to migrate to the new one. Although there were teething problems on change-over day (as there always is with technology), the staff members addressed the problems positively because they understood how important the overall transition was, and the transition achieved its goals.

With another client in the software industry, the organization faced the challenge of rolling out the global strategy across the Asia–Pacific region. After completing an implementation assessment, we discovered that the largest challenge they faced was to convince people that a new strategy was required. The organization dominated its market and was making tremendous profits. Many of the staff were thinking, "If it isn't broken, don't fix it." The leadership, however, had identified that across the seven main business lines, they were starting to lose market share and that customer satisfaction was dangerously low, especially compared to the competition. The new strategy was targeted at enhancing the business and improving customer satisfaction by turning around the key indicators and impacting every part of the business. It required the support and involvement of every staff member.

To initiate the implementation in the Asia–Pacific region, the team took the unusual (and very successful) step of running a three-week teaser campaign to launch the strategy. Each week, a different image was sent to every back office with a brief e-mail from the head of the strategy for the region. The first image, for example, was a plane flying into some clouds with copy that read, "Flying high today but notice the turbulence just ahead." None of the posters or e-mail messages explained the whole picture, and the reaction from the region was one of great curiosity. By the third week, the regional head was inundated with e-mail, calls, and people knocking on her door to find out what was going on.

A final image was sent that encapsulated what the new global strategy was and why it was being adopted. The image, of course, crossed the many language and cultural barriers of the Asia–Pacific. The final result was that the new strategy was rapidly adopted because the staff members understood why.

It is the leaders' responsibility to identify the right way to launch a strategy that works in the culture of their organization. In some organizations, a slogan is used instead of an image. When Bill Clinton was running for president of the United States, he branded his whole campaign with, "It's the economy, stupid!"

The right branding will ensure that staff members understand why the new strategy is important to lay the platform for driving the required behaviors and actions.

Summary—Leaders' Role in Implementation

Two things leaders must do differently:

1. **Be clear. Strategy cannot be implemented if it cannot be understood, and it cannot be understood if it cannot be explained.**

   When the Biz Case is not a specific item for leaders to address, then it does not receive the right amount of attention. As a result, the implementation starts off badly as staff members do not care and have no reason to be concerned with the organization's future. The goal of the Biz Case is to present the strategy in a format that is easy to understand and encourages staff members to become engaged in executing it. The challenge for the leadership team is to explain its implications to every staff member, as staff members must understand it before they can deliver on it.

2. **Brand the strategy.**

   When leaders present the strategy to the Board, it is naturally a more left-brain argument supported by projections, graphs, and a strategy paper. Taking the strategy to the whole organization requires a more right-brain argument, supported by an internal branding that captures the essence of the strategy in images and taglines.

Leaders often seem to follow an unwritten rule that the more confusing the strategy, the better it is! On the contrary, no matter how complicated the strategy, leaders must find a way for it to be easily understood by the organization. This challenge is habitually underestimated.

To brand a strategy, first identify the core messages—perhaps one; no more than four—and then translate them into visual images and a tagline.

Leaders are responsible for identifying the right way to launch a strategy—the way that works in the culture of their organization.

5

COMMUNICATE

Leaders must communicate a million complicated things if they fail to communicate a few simple and profound things.
—Boyd Clarke and Ron Crossland, authors of *The Leader's Voice*

I forget what I hear
I remember what I see
I learn what I do

—Chinese Proverb

The greatest problem with communication is the illusion that it has been accomplished.
—George Bernard Shaw, 19th-century author

The term and implications of being "dead serious" are truly thought provoking!
—Jae Pierce-Baba, CEO of LipShtick Productions and humorologist

W hen I ask groups of executives why implementation has failed in the past, one common answer is "poor communication." If leaders know this, why do they still fail to communicate properly? Strategy is designed at the top, but implemented from the bottom. Communication is the link to make this happen.

On any given day, in some city somewhere in the world, a CEO will approach the podium at the center of a stage. There will be a hush as everyone leans forward with anticipation. The CEO will announce with fanfare the new strategy, presenting a multimedia exhibit. Posters will go up around the back offices and everyone who attends will receive a coffee mug with the new strategy caption printed on it.

The day after meeting the CEO, how many staff members will have started to adopt the new strategy?

Many organizations have had an initial fanfare of a town hall meeting or multimedia presentation or something similar. After the initial fanfare, the problem is that very little tends to be communicated, and as a result staff members do not adopt it. In the implementation successes I studied, I found four important patterns that I will discuss in detail in this chapter: First, the leaders are the voice of the strategy; second, the strategy message is sticky; third, the communications is consistent and coherent; and fourth, a balance is found between old and new media.

Voice of the Strategy

When you communicate your strategy, what is your goal? It is not simply to ensure that everyone knows what the strategy is!

Although knowing the strategy is important, it is not the sole goal of the leaders' communications. The complete goal of communication goes beyond awareness of the strategy to make sure that everyone knows what to do to implement it, and that everyone is motivated to do so. Leaders must become the *voice* of the strategy, using every opportunity to explain it and make it inspiring. As in an election campaign, leaders must keep repeating the message and stay on the message. Once everyone has heard, understood, and started to act on it, management can shift from repeating the message to sharing what is happening.

Engagement is a central imperative of implementation and it is the leaders' role to initiate the engagement. Leaders must inspire staff members to want to become involved by the communication. They must demonstrate clearly how staff members can be involved and ensure they understand the message.

If you hold a town hall meeting to launch the strategy, this should be just one of many activities. There is a marketing rule called "7×7," which is a shorthand way of saying, "Give people the message seven times in seven different ways." People must hear the message numerous times in different ways, as different as they will notice different things every time they hear it. The same goes for strategy.

While communicating the strategy and its implementation, leaders must find as many ways as they can to repeat the core messages. Leaders must also be visible throughout the organization. Staff members won't adopt a strategy until they know about it and remember it. Hosting a town hall meeting or sending an e-mail isn't enough. Leaders can also for example:

- Print a newsletter.
- Celebrate a hero.
- Mention the topic at the start of every meeting for three months.
- Create a hologram of the message.
- Pass out a token that symbolizes the message (for example, if the message is about on-time delivery, give everyone a watch).
- Attend divisional off-sites.
- Create a blog to discuss the strategy with staff members.
- Go for lunch with departments.
- Host roundtable discussions on the strategy and its implementation, and what they want people to do differently.

In communication, as the saying goes, the medium is the message—and when communicating strategy implementation, the leaders are the medium. When leaders become the voice of the strategy, it demonstrates to the whole organization not only the importance of the strategy but also the continued focus of the leadership on its implementation. When leaders repeat the message through different media, this constantly reinforces its importance to staff members.

It is ironic that in many organizations, while crafting the strategy, the leadership always has implementation at the top of the to-do list, yet within six months, it can have completely vanished from the list! When leaders take their eyes off of the implementation, so do staff members.

To communicate strategy, the leaders' objective is to break the pattern of normal information flow across the organization and find different ways to communicate. They must use every opportunity to shout the message for at least three months. They must also be very visible.

The list of activities for leaders as the "voices of strategy" is numerous, and at the end of the day, there is no right combination. It is necessary to find out and do what works for each specific organization.

Sticky Strategy Message

A sticky idea is one that people understand when they hear it, that they remember later on, and that changes something about the way they think or act. That is a high standard. Think back to the last presentation you saw. How much do you remember? How did it change the decisions you make from day to day?

Leaders will spend weeks or months coming up with the right idea, but then spend only a few hours thinking about how to convey that idea to everybody else. That's a tragedy. It's worth spending time making sure that the light bulb that has gone on inside your head also goes on inside the heads of your audience, whether customers or staff members.

Hollywood director Garry Marshall (of *Pretty Woman*) once told a Maui Writers Conference audience:[1]

> Film directors know that if people walk out of your movie repeating a phrase they heard, that movie will make money. It means audience members are taking the movie home with them. They're talking about it around the office water-cooler and to their friends; which means they're serving as free word-of-mouth advertisers for you.

When you speak, do audience members walk out repeating something specific you said? When people finish reading your article, book, or blog, do they tell others about a suggestion you shared? If not, everything you said or wrote just disappeared. People might as well not have heard or read it because if they can't remember it, what good is it?

The concept of sticky messages has been developed by Chip Heath, Professor of Organizational Behavior in the Graduate School of Business at Stanford University, and Dan Heath, consultant at Duke Corporate Education.

Crafting a message that sticks: An interview with Chip Heath

The key to effective communication: make it simple, make it concrete, and make it surprising.

Lenny T. Mendonca and Matt Miller
November 2007

The ability to craft and deliver messages that influence employees, markets, and other stakeholders may seem like a mysterious talent that some people have and some don't. Jack Welch, for example, created ideas that inspired hundreds of thousands of GE employees. But many other leaders are frustrated to find that key messages sent one day are forgotten the next—or that stakeholders don't know how to interpret them.

Why do some ideas succeed while others fail? Chip Heath, professor of organizational behavior in Stanford University's Graduate School of Business, has spent the past decade seeking answers to that question. His research has ranged from the problem of what makes beliefs—urban legends, for instance—survive in the social marketplace of competing ideas to experiments that show how winning ideas emerge in populations, businesses, and other organizations. Earlier this year Heath published his findings in *Made to Stick: Why Some Ideas Survive and Others Die*,[1] written with his brother, Dan, who founded a business that specializes in this very subject.

In July 2007 Chip Heath spoke with Lenny Mendonca, a director in McKinsey's San Francisco office; Matt Miller, an adviser to McKinsey; and Parth Tewari, who was then a Sloan fellow at the Stanford Graduate School of Business, about the key principles for making an idea "stick" and how executives can use them to communicate more successfully. The conversation took place at Stanford.

---

[1]New York: Random House, 2007

The *Quarterly*: Let's start by defining success. What is a sticky idea?

Chip Heath: A sticky idea is one that people understand when they hear it, that they remember later on, and that changes something about the way they think or act. That is a high standard. Think back to the last presentation you saw. How much do you remember? How did it change the decisions you make day to day?

Leaders will spend weeks or months coming up with the right idea but then spend only a few hours thinking about how to convey that message to everybody else. That's a tragedy. It's worth spending time making sure that the lightbulb that has gone on inside your head also goes on inside the heads of your employees or customers.

The *Quarterly*: Give us an example of a sticky idea.

Chip Heath: John F. Kennedy, in 1961, proposed to put an American on the moon in a decade. That idea stuck. It motivated thousands of people across dozens of organizations, public and private. It was an unexpected idea: it got people's attention because it was so surprising—the moon is a long way up. It appealed to our emotions: we were in the Cold War and the Russians had launched the Sputnik space satellite four years earlier. It was concrete: everybody could picture what success would look like in the same way. How many goals in your organization are pictured in exactly the same way by everyone involved?

My father worked for IBM during that period. He did some of the programming on the original Gemini space missions. And he didn't think of himself as working for IBM—he thought of himself as helping to put an American on the moon. An accountant who lived down the street from us, who worked for a defense contractor, also thought of himself as helping to put an American on the moon. When you inspire the accountants you know you're onto something.

The *Quarterly*: But when is it important for ideas to have this kind of clout and when not? Surely, not every message that leaders convey should be designed to stick?

Chip Heath: True, not every message is worth obsessing over. The daily status update doesn't need to stick. But think of the messages that do: messages about your organization's strategy need to be compelling to your employees. Messages about your products and services need to convince your customers.

It's worth taking time to design a message when it needs to persist over time. If you're going to be in the room when your customer makes a buying decision or your employees make an important business decision, your message doesn't need to stick with them. But if you need people to make the right decision a week or a month later, you'd better hope your message has stuck.

The *Quarterly*: What's the hardest thing for leaders to learn about making their messages stick?

Chip Heath: I think simplicity is the hardest. Leaders know lots of things about their organization and business and want to share them all. But effective leaders are masters of simplicity. I'm not talking about dumbing down a message or turning it into a sound bite; I'm talking about identifying the most central, core elements of strategies and highlighting them. That way everyone in the company can keep their eye on the right ball. Getting the right simple message is hard to do, but you can't avoid doing it. I worked with a nonprofit organization that had *eight* core values. Research has shown that even a few good choices can paralyze people and prevent them from making a decision. How are you going to avoid decision paralysis when you're juggling eight core values? The guiding message of Bill Clinton's first presidential race was, "It's the economy, stupid." There were lots of issues in that race, but you can't keep a complicated campaign organization on track if you try to tackle all of them. You have to pick your battle and win it.

The *Quarterly*: But you've written that simplicity isn't enough—to stick, messages also have to be concrete. Please talk about the importance of that.

Chip Heath: Take an abstract message, like "Maximize shareholder value." What should one of your employees do tomorrow to make that happen?

Now contrast that abstraction with the stories told at FedEx. One of them features a driver who couldn't open one of the pickup boxes on his route—he'd left the key back at the office. His deadline was tight and he knew that by the time he could get his key and return to the box, the packages in it were going to miss the plane. So he got a wrench, quickly unbolted the whole box, and muscled it onto his truck, knowing he'd be able to unlock it back at the office! That's the kind of behavior you want when your competitive advantage is "absolute, positive reliability." That's how you're going to maximize shareholder value in the long run. But telling FedEx drivers to maximize shareholder value just leaves them hanging. The story tells them how to act.

When messages are abstract, it's frequently because a leader is suffering from the "curse of knowledge." Psychologists and behavioral economists have shown that when we know a lot about a field it becomes really tough for us to imagine what it's like *not* to know what we know—that's the curse of knowledge. If you've ever had a conversation with your IT person about what's wrong with your computer, you've been on the other side of the curse of knowledge. The IT person knows so much that he or she can't imagine knowing as little as the rest of us. And we're all like that IT person in our own domain of expertise: prone to be overly complex and abstract.

As an executive, you may have 30 years of experience in business and 20 years in a company. So when you talk about maximizing shareholder value, you're speaking in an abstract language you've learned to understand. But that abstraction is not going to be at all clear to your frontline employees. You're better off looking for your equivalent of the FedEx story.

The *Quarterly*: Take this a step further and show us how leaders use these ideas to create change in their organizations.

Chip Heath: When Jack Welch was turning around GE he had a number of legacy businesses in declining industries. He often told a story about a retreat he had with the managers of the nuclear-engineering group. This was after the 1979 meltdown at the Three Mile Island nuclear-power station, yet their business plan still assumed that they would continue to sell more nuclear-power plants in the United States. He said to them, "I can't imagine we're ever going to sell another nuclear-power plant, so go back and make this plan work without selling new reactors." They went back and developed a plan based on selling services to existing reactors.

He used that story with managers in other legacy units. They could recognize that the managers of the nuclear group were deluded about selling more product, and maybe that prompted them to ask themselves if they were deluded too. And it was a story that provided a concrete suggestion—you could build a great business selling to an existing base.

When you come up with a concrete story like that, you're in a good position to change the way people think and behave.

The *Quarterly*: How do you adapt ideas that make sense in the boardroom to other audiences, such as employees, the business community, and the broader social sphere?

Chip Heath: When ideas share the properties of sticky ideas—simplicity, concreteness, stories—they are more portable. Jack Welch could take his story about the nuclear group to lots of audiences. He could use it with Wall Street analysts who were worried about GE's business mix to tell them why GE was still a good bet. He could use it with employees who were worried about the industries they were in to reassure them that there's hope for a good business even in the lousiest industry. Leaders constantly have to talk to audiences who have many different agendas. A good story or example is going to be way more portable across those audiences than an industry analysis or a net present value calculation or a seven-point change plan.

The *Quarterly*: Is the ability to design sticky messages learnable?

Chip Heath: Yes, it is. Steve Jobs looks like a natural, but he's known in Silicon Valley for the obsessive amounts of time he spends working on his new-product introductions. He thinks systematically about his messages and most of them work. But few other leaders are as deliberate.

If you want to learn how to make your messages stick, the highest-return-on-investment advice is to be more concrete. Systematically go through your speech, your PowerPoint deck, or your memo and strike out every abstraction. Instead of saying "outstanding customer service," substitute an example. At Nordstrom they give the example of the salesperson who gift-wrapped a package a customer bought at Macy's. Now all of a sudden the abstraction about outstanding customer service becomes meaningful for a Nordstrom audience. You will improve your communication ability by 200 or 300 percent.

Often, leaders think that to make their messages stick they have to come up with a slogan worthy of Madison Avenue. But if you think about most commercials, they're actually not very sticky. That's why we have to repeat them so many times. Compare the typical ad tagline with the FedEx story about the driver who unbolted the box when he forgot his key. That story has the sticking power of an urban legend, yet it's true. It's a concrete example that embodies the strategy of absolute reliability. You can tell it to your employees to guide them on how to act. And you use it in a commercial that's probably much better than the typical FedEx commercial at motivating customers to trust FedEx—those people are fanatical about reliability.

The *Quarterly*: What role do market research and focus groups play in designing sticky messages?

Chip Heath: I'm a big fan of research because I'm a researcher. But let's face it: many of the most important messages in your organization never get near a focus group. I've never heard about a top leadership team that pitched a strategy presentation to a focus group.

You can get a long way toward a sticky message just by building in the right properties. Is my message simple enough? Is it concrete? Is there a story I could tell? If leaders want to get something done in an organization of 1,000 or 10,000 or 100,000, they'd better spend some time working through the checklist of traits that make a message sticky. And if on top of that you hold a focus group for the new-strategy speech with a random sample of employees from across your organization, their feedback will improve your message even more. You'll be able to see faces light up when you hit the right example.

The *Quarterly*: What does Marshall McLuhan's famous phrase "the medium is the message" mean today? How important is the medium in all this?

Chip Heath: I admire McLuhan for coming up with a sticky slogan, but with all due respect his slogan is wrong. In truth, the message is the message. People who think too much about the medium—opt-in newsletters, the Internet, Web 2.0—are making the same mistake that people have made for years in education. Remember how the 8-millimeter film was going to revolutionize education? Then the VCR? Then the personal computer? The medium can certainly help, but an 8-millimeter film didn't salvage a bad math lesson.

Leaders should take comfort that when they find some good stories to tell, the medium doesn't matter. Think about Seabiscuit, the undersized horse who became a champion. That story about overcoming adversity inspired people in the 1930s who read about it in the newspapers. It inspired people in the 2000s no matter whether they read the book or saw the movie. If you have the money to produce a movie about your inspiring story of organizational renewal, that's great. If not, just find an inspiring story and put it in your newsletter.

Six Basic Traits

Chip Heath's research suggests that sticky ideas share six basic traits.

1. *Simplicity*. Messages are most memorable if they are short and deep. Glib sound bites are short, but they don't last. Proverbs such as the golden rule are short but also deep enough to guide the behavior of people over generations.

2. *Unexpectedness*. Something that sounds like common sense won't stick. Look for the parts of your message that are uncommon sense. Such messages generate interest and curiosity.

3. *Concreteness*. Abstract language and ideas don't leave sensory impressions; concrete images do. Compare "get an American on the moon in this decade" with "seize leadership in the space race through targeted technology initiatives and enhanced team-based routines."

4. *Credibility*. Will the audience buy the message? Can a case be made for the message or is it a confabulation of spin? Very often, a person trying to convey a message cites outside experts when the most credible source is the person listening to the message. Questions—"Have you experienced this?"—are often more credible than outside experts.

5. *Emotions*. Case studies that involve people also move them. "We are wired," Heath writes, "to feel things for people, not abstractions."

6. *Stories*. We all tell stories every day. Why? "Research shows that mentally rehearsing a situation helps us perform better when we encounter that situation," Heath writes. "Stories act as a kind of mental flight simulator, preparing us to respond more quickly and effectively."

I'm especially fond of Chip's observations regarding JFK's statement about putting a man on the moon. In *Made to Stick,* he and Dan Heath go even further than in the list of basic traits, rewriting the statement as if it had been written by a CEO: "Our mission is to become the international leader in the space industry through maximum team-centered innovation and strategically targeted aerospace initiatives"![2]

Consistent, Coherent Communication

After the initial fanfare in many organizations, the communication about a strategy often becomes unstructured and ad hoc. It is typically left to the HR or Communication Department to send out messages when they feel appropriate. As a result, the rest of the organization does not know what is happening—and worse, starts to lose interest. The main messages being sent concern milestones met and successes achieved. Newsletters are created and random e-mails sent out. What is needed is a consistent, coherent, and structured communication.

Leaders must build on the initial excitement and fan the flames. Structured communication should be conducted targeting different groups with selected messages designed to accomplish the following objectives:

1. Regularly update staff members on the progress of the implementation.
2. Share success stories and lessons learned from failures.
3. Provide updates of upcoming activities, changes, and developments.
4. Share news of the strategy's impact on the business, customer, and operations.
5. Ensure staff members remain engaged in the implementation and take the right actions.

While overseeing the messages being sent out, leaders should ensure consistency. This means providing regular updates based on the five objectives I just listed. Keeping communications consistent keeps the implementation on the minds of staff members, as well as keeping them informed.

While overseeing the messages being sent out and monitoring their consistency, leaders should also ensure they are coherent. Keep in mind that the 10 Commandments is only 173 words, the Gettysburg Address is 272 words and takes four minutes to say, the Declaration of Independence contains 300 words, and a standard memo to boost organizational productivity contains 2,000 words! Adopt the best practices discussed in the SUCCES model in the section "Six Basic Traits" and be concise and specific.

In *Bricks to Bridges,* I explained how leaders tend to use KICC instead of KISS (Keep It Complicated and Confusing rather than Keep It Simple and Short). This is especially true around strategy, where many leaders feel that if it is not complex, then it is not a good strategy. Part of the goal of the communication is to encourage staff members to participate in the implementation. The more coherent the message, the more easily it will enlist support.

In business, leaders tend to overcomplicate communication, making it hard for people to understand the simplest of messages. The leader's goal in communicating a new strategy is to enable staff members to understand what's changing, explain why the organization is changing, and define what people should do differently.

Yet to communicate these simple messages, leaders frequently adopt ambiguous terms, blurring the implementation's objectives and goals and leaving people confused and baffled. For example, "By adopting our new strategy, we will be shifting the business away from our traditional offering to our old market and opening up new opportunities in untapped markets that will win over a new client based on our fast turnaround times, excellent product, and innovative response." Statements like this leave staff confused and give birth to comments such as, "Our CEO talks too much about too little!" When they finally do translate its meaning into their own language, it comes out as *more work, same pay!*

Communication must be simple, engaging, and easy to understand. Key messages about the new strategy should be communicated in different ways because different people have different ways of learning. The leaders' role is to ensure that the strategy is translated into actions that everyone in the organization can undertake.

An acid test of successful communication is to check to see what leaders are discussing with their teams. If it is how they can act on the strategy, then the communication is working. If it is about operational challenges or staff turnover, or how to save costs, then it is not working.

Implementing strategy successfully means changing the conversations in the organization. It is estimated, from Bridges research, that in a weekly leadership meeting, the team spends 85 percent of its time discussing operations and only 15 percent on strategy. To successfully implement strategy, this must be reversed. Part of the way to achieve the reverse is to manage the communication, and specifically the agenda and discussions at meetings. For example, start every leadership meeting with a review of the Balanced Scorecard or have the leaders ask their staff members every week, "What actions have you taken this week to make the strategy come alive?"

Staff members are bombarded daily with messages. It is estimated that currently

- 60 billion e-mails are sent each day.
- 23 billion instant messages are sent each day.

This places even more emphasis on ensuring that the strategy message is heard consistently and coherently.

Old Media versus New Media

Communicate to your staff the same way your kids communicate to their friends!

The world of media is changing, and most of us in leadership positions or acting as advisers are just on the periphery of the new world. Many leaders are lagging behind the new forms of media; if they're learning, it is their children who are teaching them. Web 2.0, which includes, for example, blogs, Twitter, IM (Instant Messaging), MySpace, Facebook and Wiki are now becoming common language and more important popular forms of communication. Yet when most leaders communicate their strategy, they rely on old media—newsletters, posters, and town hall meetings.

When communicating your strategy, you must not ignore the way staff members are communicating outside the office. Remember that the first goal of communication is for staff members to know and understand the strategy (then to know what to do and be motivated to do it). You have a responsibility to reach your staff members in their preferred medium, not yours. A blog, for example, provides an excellent platform for staff members to not only read about the strategy online but also to communicate back to you on the implementation journey. It is also easy to update and manage. Reflect for a moment on how much effort goes into publishing a corporate newsletter and immediately the benefits of a blog can start to be understood. Visit the Bridges blog at http://strategyimplementation.blogspot.com as an example.

Twitter is also rapidly growing in popularity and is a very fast and easy way to communicate as the story in the sidebar demonstrates.

On-the-Spot News

Early in 2009, the pilot of a commercial airliner with both engines knocked out saved the lives of every passenger on board by crash landing in the Hudson River in New York. When the plane hit the water, a bystander took a picture on his cell phone and immediately uploaded the picture to Twitpic, the Twitter photo service. Before any of the global TV news channels were reporting the story, thousands of people had received the picture of the crash.

The right balance must be found between old and new media. Old media should not be ignored. A hint is to watch your own kids and their habits. How much time do they spend reading magazines as against surfing the Web for information? What is the balance between calling their friends and IM? Do they have their own blogs?

When planning to communicate your strategy, in addition to the old media, consider these outlets:

1. Create a blog on your strategy and ask staff members to contribute their thoughts to it. A blog is a couple of pages and should start off explaining what the strategy is, why it is important for the organization to adopt it. It should then be specific about what you want staff members to do. Every few weeks a new blog entry should be posted introducing specific details about the strategy roll-out. Place a link to the blog on your corporate Web site.

2. Use Twitter to allow your team to know what is important to you, where you are, and what you are working on. Don't use Twitter as a minute-by-minute diary of your life. Twitter is micro blogging, and when used correctly is a powerful tool. When it is abused it becomes a nuisance. Use it to let your followers know what you are doing to execute the strategy. As an example, check out my Twitter page at http://twitter.com/speculand.

3. Upload a video onto YouTube and send the link to staff members. This can be a video clip of the town hall meeting you presented or a specially shot clip. Keep the clip to less than four minutes. Fight the temptation to upload your corporate video.

4. Host an Internet town hall meeting. President Obama, a naturally talented speaker, has excelled in adopting new media and especially Internet town hall meetings. If you are leading a global organization, this is a great way to talk to staff members around the world.

5. Initiate discussions in chat rooms on the challenges staff members are having in implementing the strategy. When Michael Dell came back as CEO of his company he wanted to improve Dell laptops to make them more customer friendly. Dell went online to talk to customers directly in chat rooms. The suggestions, such as lights behind the keyboards, were immediately adopted and sales increased.

In the next chapter I discuss how to measure your implementation. New media reflects the mind shift leaders must have to successfully implement strategy. For example, to measure new media it is not about ROI but the number exposed to the new strategy; the number of people visiting the strategy blog, number of strategy blog comments and the quality of their comments; or the number of people viewing your video on YouTube. Just like the medium, measures are changing.

Summary—Leaders' Role in Implementation

Four things leaders must do differently:

1. **Become the voice of the strategy.**
   It is most important for many organizations to shift the focus in communication from creating awareness of what the strategy is about to explaining the goal of the communication to make sure everyone knows the strategy, knows what to do to implement it, and is motivated to do it. Achieving this shift entails a complete repositioning and change in communication objectives and positioning.

   "Voice of the strategy" leaders need to spend a minimum of three months shouting the strategy across the whole organization, no matter the size of the organization. Communicate the message in as many different ways as possible and use every opportunity to personally be the medium.

   After three months, leaders can check with their frontline staff to see if they know what the strategy is, how they can contribute to it, and if they are motivated to do so.

   The list of activities for leaders as the "voice of the strategy" is endless, and at the end of the day there is no right combination. It is essential to find out what works best in each organization.

2. **Create a sticky strategy message by adopting the SUCCES model.**
   A sticky idea is one that people understand when they hear it, that they remember later on, and that changes something about the way they think or act.

   Chip Heath's research suggests that sticky ideas share six basic traits:

Simplicity. Messages are most memorable if they are short and deep.

Unexpectedness. Look for the parts of your message that are uncommon sense. Such messages generate interest and curiosity.

Concreteness. Use concrete images that grab attention and stay with the audience.

Credibility. Build your case carefully, and use questions about the audience's experience.

Emotions. Use case studies that involve people and also move them.

Stories. Tell stories to help people understand at a gut level what they need to do.

3. **Make sure the communication is consistent and coherent.**

   After the initial fanfare in many organizations, communication about a strategy often becomes unstructured and ad hoc. Leaders must make sure that communication goes beyond the initial fanfare and provides a consistent and coherent structured message about not only how the implementation is progressing, but also the successes, customer feedback, and what is going to happen next.

   The communication message must be targeted at different groups, as different groups require different amounts of information. In addition, leaders must make sure that the conversation with their direct reports is changing, and that in meetings and everyday conversations they are discussing how to implement the strategy.

4. **Balance new media and old media.**

   Leaders must adopt a balance between new media and old media to communicate strategy. The balance will depend on the audience—for example, if staff members are mostly working on the factory floor, then old media will be more prevalent. If most of the staff members are addicted to their BlackBerrys, then you need to be blogging and sending tweets. When adopting new media—Web 2.0—consider how your staff members communicate outside work and then plan your communication accordingly, using media such as blogs, Twitter, YouTube, and chat rooms as needed.

Endnotes

1 Quoted by Sam Horn; accessed at http://samhornpop.wordpress.com/2008/03/10/whats-your-money-phrase/, June 5, 2009.

2 Chip Heath and Dan Heath, *Made to Stick* (New York: Random House, 2008).

6

MEASURE

Get your facts first, and then you can distort them as much as you please.

—Mark Twain

When you can measure what you are speaking about and express it in numbers you know something about it; but when you cannot measure it, when you cannot express it in numbers, your knowledge is of a meager and unsatisfactory kind.

—Lord Kelvin, 1850s

There are two key messages for leaders to consider under Measure on the Implementation Compass. The first is that most organizations are using the wrong measures to track their strategy and the second is that measures drive behavior. The objective of this chapter is to understand how critical it is for leaders to have the right measures to track the implementation of the strategy.

Using the Wrong Measures to Track Strategy

When leaders launch a new strategy they must stop using the measures that track old strategies and start to create new measures to track the new strategy. Although this is both logical and sensible, it does not happen. I am still stunned by how many global organizations change their strategy, but do not change their measures.

> Knowing what to measure and how to measure it makes a complicated world much less so. If you learn how to look at data in the right way, you can explain riddles that otherwise might have seemed impossible. Because there is nothing like the sheer power of numbers to scrub away layers of confusion and contradiction.
> —Steven D. Levitt, economist and author

I once worked with a CEO who had just adopted a new strategy in an emerging market. At the heart of the strategy was customer service, which was still a differentiator in his market. When I asked what measures he was using to track organization-wide customer service, he did not have even one! He had no way of measuring the key component of the strategy. As we know, staff members are smart. They work on what gets measured, not what leaders say. In the organization, staff members did not focus on service as it was not measured. Measures must support the strategy, but in many organizations this does not happen.

Current Measures, Obsolete or Not?

Many measures used in organizations today are obsolete. Despite the importance of intangible assets, we still mostly measure tangible assets. For example, consider the expression, "People are our most important asset." This statement in itself is not only wrong, but also reveals the need for measures to be updated.

First, people in general are not your most important asset; the right people—the mavericks—are your most important asset.

Second, any staff members who can read the annual report will look at the right-hand side of the balance sheet, and even worse than not seeing people listed as an asset, they will see that what is more valuable to the organization is the chairs they are sitting on and the computer they are using! They will look at the profit and loss statement and see that people are measured as an expense! There is a major disconnect between what leaders say and what they measure, and this contributes to the downfall of the implementation.

Baruch Lev of the Brookings Institution indicates that in 1982, 62 percent of the market value (measured by market capitalization) of organizations could be attributed to tangible assets and only 38 percent to intangibles. Ten years later, the Brookings analysis of S&P 500 organizations showed that the relationship had been reversed: in 1992, it was 32 percent tangible to 68 percent intangible.[1]

A follow-up study in 1998 showed that, with the rise of the knowledge-based economy, the ratio had further shifted to 85 percent intangible to 15 percent tangible.[2]

We must therefore develop measures that reflect both tangible and intangible. Too many organizations are dependent on financial measures.

On the Implementation Compass, Measure addresses the specific KPIs leaders must identify and adopt to track the strategy and its implementation.

With many clients, Measure is the first step of the implementation journey. This is because when I meet with leaders one-on-one, I generally discover that they lack a shared understanding of their strategy. Many of them cannot articulate what the strategy means to their individual areas of responsibility. They have not identified the actions they expect from their team members, and so, unsurprisingly, they do not have targeted strategic measures in place. Measure allows leaders to translate the strategy into objectives, measures, and actions.

Kaplan and Norton have achieved phenomenal breakthroughs in this area, and if you are looking to change your measures, I recommend adopting a Strategy Map and the Balanced Scorecard.

Strategy Maps and the Balanced Scorecard

50% of organizations who claim to be using the Balance Scorecard are doing it wrong, for example, no executive ownership, scorecard not linked to strategy or management process.
—Kaplan and Norton

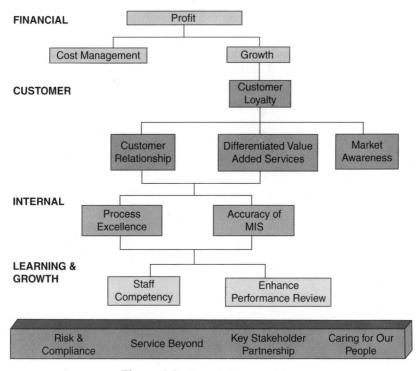

Figure 6.1 Sample Strategy Map.

Strategy Maps, created by Kaplan and Norton, provide a one-page summary of the strategy and the objectives under four headings: Learning & Growth, Internal Process, Customer, and Financial. The Strategy Map drives the creation of the Scorecard. The leadership team identifies at least one measure for each objective and sets targets. During this stage, leaders grasp further clarification of the strategy's impact on business units.

Figure 6.1 is a sample of the Strategy Maps we prepare at Bridges.

The methodology for creating a Strategy Map and the Balanced Scorecard is not complicated. A good consultant can facilitate the process over a couple of months, combining onsite interviews and meetings with leadership workshops. The real challenge is not in crafting the map and scorecard but in adopting them.

Creating the Strategy Map and Balanced Scorecard

Many organizations engage external consultants to facilitate the discussions to create a Strategy Map and Balanced Scorecard. Although it is not a complicated process, there are plenty of potential problems, discussions on methodology, and templates that a consultant can resolve.

The consultant typically meets with the leaders to conduct one-on-one interviews and with the staff members to obtain a bottom-up perspective. At the end of the interviews and after a review of the strategy, business, and organization, the consultant has the first draft of the Strategy Map.

The leadership team then meets for a two-day offsite and refines the first draft of the map. The reason the consultant creates the first draft is to accelerate the process. Also, the objective is not to teach the leaders how to create a Strategy Map, but to translate the big-picture strategy into strategic objectives in the four areas—Learning & Growth, Internal Process, Customer, and Financial, and draw the cause-and-effect relationships among the objectives.

It should be noted that the four headings can be changed when required. For example, a nonprofit organization would have Mission on top and not Financials.

After a two-week break to reflect on the map, the team will meet again for another two-day offsite. The focus is to identify at least one measure per strategic objective, and to identify the targets and baseline data.

The final step is to work on actions at two levels. The first level is the actions required to implement the Balanced Scorecard; for example, you might need to gather baseline data for a new measure or create a new measure. The second level is the actions required to implement the strategy based on a review of the strategic objectives and measures; for example, install an organization-wide employee satisfaction index.

The challenge then becomes tougher as you move from discussions to doing. The challenge in adopting the Balanced Scorecard as a management tool is a hurdle that many leaders fail as they underestimate the effort required. The Balanced Scorecard must drive leadership discussions, that is, it must be actively reviewed and acted upon.

One CEO we worked with immediately changed the way he ran his senior management meetings after creating the Strategy Map and Balanced Scorecard. He started every meeting with a review of the map and then a discussion on the measures and actions.

This shifted the conversation from operations to strategy and reinforced the importance of adopting the new strategy to the rest of the organization.

This had the desired effect of shifting the conversation among his direct reports from 85 percent operational and only 15 percent strategic to vice versa. In addition, the impact also cascaded down to middle managers, who started to adopt the new strategy and measures.

The effort involved in adopting the Balanced Scorecard should not be underestimated. It takes a singular focus and staying power that must be led by the senior leadership.

Once the scorecard is adopted, you must consider the impact the measures have on your staff members, because measures drive behaviors.

Measures Drive Behavior

When creating the Strategy Map and the Balanced Scorecard, leaders must pay specific attention to the selection of the measures and the behaviors they drive. This starts with reviewing the measures as they are created and asking "What behavior do we expect to see from staff members when they adopt these measures?" These conclusions need to be followed up via management by walking around to ensure the measures are really driving the behavior they expect to see.

Measures do not always drive the behaviors that leaders expect, as the four stories in the sidebar "You Get What You Measure" illustrate.

You Get What You Measure

1. Chicken Efficiency

The outlet managers of a fast food chain paid only lip service to many of the chain management's measures. This is because they knew the only measurement that anyone checked rigorously was how much cooked chicken each outlet threw away at the end of the day—a measure they called Chicken Efficiency.

Naturally, outlet managers focused on keeping their bosses happy. To hit their Chicken Efficiency targets; they simply didn't cook any chicken until somebody ordered it! If management, however, had measured a composite of indicators, they would have found that customers were waiting up to 20 minutes for their meals. Many customers became so dissatisfied with the "fast" food service that they never returned. But at least the outlet managers hit their targets!

It is important that after selecting measures, leaders check on the impact they are having across the organization.

2. Longer Customer Waiting Time

A consumer bank head introduced new measures to track revenue and cross-selling of products. He later observed that in some branches, the staff members behind the counter were not serving some customers, and that the waiting times were becoming longer. On closer inspection and after discussion with the branch staff he discovered that because the staff members were mostly measured on their financial and cross-sell ratio measures, they were only serving the customers who looked as if they could contribute toward their targets. If someone was poorly dressed, then the service staff ignored them by not calling them forward and waited for someone else to serve who looked more promising.

3. Shoot the Doctor

In Russia, the czar discovered that the most disease-ridden province in his empire was also the one with the most doctors. The solution? He promptly ordered all the doctors shot dead. This does not mean you shoot the divisional manager with the worst performance, but that understanding metrics and correlation is not easy.

4. National Library Board

In Singapore, the National Library Board has become a global benchmark on how to run a library, and its staff frequently entertains visitors to share their success. In the 1990s, the leadership recognized a disconnect between their mission of getting as many people as possible to read in Singapore and the measures they were using. The team revisited its measurement system so as to encourage the right behaviors.

To encourage the public, they started to measure the number of books borrowed per member and the turnover rate for books. In addition, the librarians responded by also adopting many measures aimed at encouraging more people to read and borrow books.

In the next step, the leadership reviewed the processes that supported the measures and changed them again to build further support for their mission. For example, they allowed customers to borrow books from one library and return them to another, as well as setting up stations at post offices and supermarkets for book returns. They also went online to allow readers to borrow in advance and pick up books once available at a library of their choice.

It is imperative that when leaders create measures, they consider their impact and constantly review the behavior of staff members.

Complexity of Measures

In addition to considering the behavior measures will drive, also consider the complexity of the measure. When identifying measures, leaders can be very imaginative, but there may be a high cost in adopting a measure. If it is too complex an alternative measure needs to be identified. For example, a fashion retailer wanted to determine the conversion ratio in its stores (the percentage of shoppers who bought something). Various complex schemes were proposed, involving the use of radio frequency identification tags and various types of sensors. In the end, the organization decided on the simple concept of hiring students to sit outside their stores and count the numbers of people who went into the store and the number coming out carrying shopping bags. The more inexpensive and convenient it is to calculate a metric, the better. You must also consider how often it needs to be calculated.

The discussion on a measure's complexity should happen when leaders are initially selecting the measure for the Balanced Scorecard. If later on they observe that adopting a measure is more troublesome than it is worth, then they must step in and consider adopting another measure or dropping the point completely.

The Right Measures

"That which is measured improves" is the old saying, but if you are measuring the wrong thing, making it better will do little or no good.

Identifying the right measures is not easy and on many occasions leaders select bad measures. Leaders must take time to reflect on the long-term impact of a measure. When creating the Strategy Map and Balanced Scorecard they should consider the following points:

- Never rely on a single metric in isolation, as numbers can be misleading. Adopt multiple metrics to give a stronger perspective.
- Consider the cause-and-effect relationship between measures from the Strategy Map. How will one measure impact another? For example, staff training should lead to higher productivity.
- Use metrics that track each of the perspectives on the Balanced Scorecard. For example, this implies focusing on supporting simultaneous optimization of cost, service, quality, and risk.
- Ensure that someone senior is responsible and accountable for each of the Balanced Scorecard metrics. This person should see that targets being met by ensuring that staff members are taking the right action.
- Check that measures are actionable. This means that the measures should provide a mechanism through which corrective action can be taken.
- Check that measures are appropriately integrated into incentive programs and reward structures. This will help to encourage desired behaviors.
- Develop measures that encourage teamwork.
- Develop measures that motivate.

Even though identifying the right measures is critical, it is linking the measures to action that makes the biggest difference and drives the implementation. During this stage, leaders must constantly review the measures to make sure they are achieving the desired impact and results.

Summary—Leaders' Role in Implementation

Four things leaders must do differently:

1. **Change the strategy, change the measures.**
   Leaders are responsible for ensuring that the organization stops measuring the old strategy and puts in place new measures for the new strategy. One of the best ways to do this is to adopt a

Strategy Map and the Balanced Scorecard. Create a Strategy Map to show the strategy on one page and translate the impact of that strategy to everyone. Show the transition from the "big think" to everyday actions.

A leader's role is to lead the Strategy Map and Balanced Scorecard development and to show everyone the importance of the new system by immediately adopting it.

2. **Remember that measures drive behavior.**
New measures drive new behaviors, and leaders need to make sure that staff member behaviors are putting the strategy into practice.

Quite often, the behaviors that the measures drive are detrimental to the strategy and the behaviors that staff members adopt are not what the leaders were anticipating. Make sure that the behaviors staff members take support the strategy.

3. **Control the complexity of measures.**
The discussion on complexity should occur when leaders initially select a measure for the Balanced Scorecard. If later on they observe that adopting a measure is more trouble than it is worth, then they must consider adopting another measure or dropping the issue completely.

4. **Measure the right things.**
"That which is measured improves" is the old saying, but if you are measuring the wrong thing, making it better will do little or no good. Identifying the right measures is not easy and on many occasions, leaders select bad measures. Leaders must take time to reflect on the long-term impact of a measure when they are creating the Strategy Map and Balanced Scorecard, and review its impact during the implementation.

Endnotes

1 B. Lev, *Intangibles: Management, Measurement, and Reporting* (Washington, DC: Brookings Institution Press, 2001).
2 Ibid.

7

CULTURE

You must create a culture of trust and commitment that motivates people to implement the strategy, not to the letter but to the spirit.

—W. Chan Kim and Renee Mauborgne, authors,
Blue Ocean Strategy

The real culture of any firm is how the employees are treated and decisions are made each and every day.

—Ron Rael, corporate culture coach

I define culture as the way we do everything in an organization. It is one of the main differentiators between you and your competition, as it is a key driver of staff members' attitudes and behaviors. It impacts, for example, how you run a meeting, where you hold your offsites, the way you launch a new product, the dress code, and the type of people you attract and retain.

One way to understand an organization's culture is to ask, "Who are the heroes and what stories do people tell about them?" According to Geoffrey Moore, an organization's culture can be defined by the kind of values it cherishes and the kinds of people, activities, and achievements it celebrates.[1] In this chapter, I examine the relationship between strategy, implementation, and culture, discussing how to lead the changing of a culture and why leaders must abandon yesterday's way of working. On the Implementation Compass, Culture is the hardest direction to implement as it involves, everything.

Strategy, Culture, and Implementation

Does strategy drive culture or culture drive strategy?

This question has been studied by leading academics around the world. Most believe that strategy drives culture because strategy is all about the organization's future and cannot be constrained or blinkered by the culture. Therefore, when developing the organization's strategy, its leaders are wise to keep an open mind and avoid limitations.

This, then, poses a second question: "What is the relationship between culture and implementation?" Culture does not drive strategy, but it does drive the way you *implement* your strategy.

This means that leaders have to identify the implementation approach that fits the culture of the organization. For example, if the implementation of the strategy moves too fast for the culture, you end up overpromising and underdelivering—and the effort crumbles. If the implementation moves too slowly for the culture, then you lose momentum and key people—the mavericks—lose interest and you fail.

Finding the right balance is not easy—as Carly Fiorina, former CEO at Hewlett-Packard, discovered the hard way. In hindsight, many will say that Fiorina had the right strategy but could not execute it. Mark Hurd, who took over from Fiorina, is regarded as an implementation specialist. He has become known for successfully executing HP strategy, part of which he inherited from his predecessor. Later in the chapter, I examine the HP situation in the case study "A Contrast in Leadership."

The leaders' role is to ensure that the culture enables the new strategy's implementation. If the current culture does not do so, they need to build a culture that reinforces implementation, as implementation is not a department—it is a culture.

Ensuring That the Culture Supports Behaviors and Actions

Once leaders have defined the strategy, they need to set their people up for success by ensuring that the culture supports the behaviors and actions they are required to take. This is done by reviewing current social norms and rituals, and often by changing many elements. After all, culture is the way we do everything in the organization and organizations are living mechanisms. If you change only one thing, it does not change the organization.

The leaders must examine the day-to-day life of the organization to make sure it drives the new strategy's implementation. For example, one leadership team in the United States noted that their meetings took too long and slowed down the implementation process. Staff members simply spent too much time talking in meetings and not enough time on the job, taking the right actions. To change this, all the chairs were taken out of the meeting rooms. All meeting attendees had to stand! This alone dramatically shortened meetings from two hours to 20 minutes, releasing time to take meaningful action.

In Malaysia, a leadership team from an organization supplying medical products noted that occasionally a leader would speak angrily to a staff member in front of others in the department. This had a negative effect on the staff member being spoken to and those nearby. Not only was it embarrassing for the target to be shouted at in public, but, in Asia, it was also a major loss of face. To stop this, the leadership team started a "code blue" policy. This meant that if, after all the leaders agreed to stop this detrimental behavior, one leader still did it, the rest would take action. They would immediately take the offending leader to the conference room, and, in front of the team, the offender would have to explain the lapse. Implementing this policy stopped the negative behavior cold.

In the last few years, companies such as Southwest Airlines have reinforced the importance of having a strong corporate culture to drive the right behaviors and actions. Southwest Airlines has a culture of "fun." Another organization that has built a strong culture to drive its strategy implementation is Zappos, founded in San Francisco in 1999. Zappos sells shoes and apparel online, and offers not only free shipping but also free 365-day returns. Based out of Las Vegas, the staff members are encouraged to provide WOW service. Most of the staff members work in the call center. They have no script to follow, as they are encouraged to be individualistic and respond to the customer on the phone. It is not unknown for a customer to receive a bunch of flowers with an order. The CEO, Tony Hsieh, leads by example—taking an annual salary of $36,000 and creating the core values of Zappos that drive the culture:

1. Deliver WOW Through Service
2. Embrace and Drive Change
3. Create Fun and A Little Weirdness
4. Be Adventurous, Creative, and Open-Minded
5. Pursue Growth and Learning
6. Build Open and Honest Relationships With Communication
7. Build a Positive Team and Family Spirit
8. Do More With Less
9. Be Passionate and Determined
10. Be Humble[2]

Leaders have a responsibility to examine the culture of the organization and ensure it is supporting the implementation.

Culture Applies Both to Organizations and to Countries

Consider that culture is not only unique to organizations but also to countries. Singapore has developed a strong culture in a relatively short time. For example, people in Singapore have strong family values. This is reinforced by giving people who buy apartments near their parents' homes a discount on the property. In addition, Singapore requires compulsory national service for young men to help them develop stronger characters. A slogan circulates throughout the country. It says, "Low crime does not mean no crime." Singapore adopts capital punishment and is one of the safest countries in the world. If you break the law, no matter who you are—a government employee or a tourist, Michael Fay, or a businessman—you will be punished harshly.

Singapore also thrives on efficiency. To control the volume of traffic, cars are expensive and taxes on cars can equal their cost. When some kids stuck chewing gum on the subway doors, it stopped the doors closing properly and slowed the trains. The government's response? In 1992, it banned chewing gum altogether—and aside from a few therapeutic uses, it's still banned to this day.

In Singapore, the culture drives and supports how the government implements its strategies.

Leadership Team Responsible for Changing the Culture

If an organization's culture needs to change to support strategy implementation, the responsibility for doing so lies with the CEO and the senior leadership team—it is a top-down job. Therefore, the leadership team should start by asking:

- What behaviors do we want staff members to adopt?
- What aspects of the culture must change to support the strategy execution? (For instance, typical meeting agendas, customer focus, changes in leadership style.)
- What supporting mechanisms will encourage these behaviors? (For example, for the call center to give fast, responsive service to customers, it needs computer technology that is fast and responsive.)
- What behaviors should the leadership team be modeling? (For example, if we want staff members to discuss and react to measures, then leaders should do so first.)
- Does the reward and recognition scheme encourage the behaviors of the new strategy?

Keep in mind that culture is forever evolving. This happens at all levels, in families as well as countries and organizations. My grandfather was poor but lived in a large hut; my father was okay and we lived in an average home. Today, I'm rich—but spend most of my life in a cubicle!

In the end, management doesn't change culture. Management invites the workforce itself to change the culture. If I could have chosen not to tackle the IBM culture head-on, I probably wouldn't have. My bias coming in was toward strategy,

analysis, and measurement. In comparison, changing the atti-
tude and behaviors of hundreds of thousands of people is very,
very hard. [Yet] I came to see in my time at IBM that culture
isn't just one aspect of the game—it is the game.
—Lou Gerstner, author of *Who Says Elephants Can't Dance*
and former CEO of IBM

A powerful example of the relationship between strategy and culture comes from Hewlett-Packard's recent activities, discussed in the case study "A Contrast in Leadership."

A Contrast in Leadership

Hewlett-Packard, an organization that constantly changes its business and strategy, has had its share of failures and successes. In the 1970s its main business was in testing and measurement. A decade later, it focused on mini-computers. Today, it specializes in printers and personal computers. Throughout all its transitions, the HP Way has prevailed.

The HP Way is the name given to the organization's strong and unique culture. For many years, the HP Way had been the benchmark for leaders from other organizations, with case studies about HP used by business schools around the world. *The HP Way* was even published as a book by one of its founders, David Packard.[3]

However, HP recently lost its way!

In 1999, Carly Fiorina took over as its CEO. She came to the position with a background in sales and with experience as a telecommunications executive at AT&T and Lucent Technologies. In 2005 she left HP in a cloud of unpopularity, coming both from within HP and outside of it. On the day she resigned, HP's stock rose 7.5 percent. Experts believe her exit hinged not on lack of vision but on poor execution of her strategy.

When Fiorina first joined HP, she worked at a rapid pace, traveling extensively and sharing her vision throughout the organization. She wanted to maintain a high-level presence with customers and staff members.

Fiorina's leadership style, though, went against the HP Way. She was a big-picture thinker who set unattainable stretch goals.

Much of her managers' time was directed at how to deliver the stretch goals rather than executing the strategy. She even refused to name a chief operating officer to help her implement the details of her strategy.

Fiorina's glamorous and flashy leadership style became an issue with some managers and staff members because of its sharp contrast to the values of the HP Way. She believed she only needed 15 percent of the people in the organization to be on board with her to succeed at executing her strategy. This proved to be a colossal mistake. She became isolated at the top and staff members were never engaged in the implementation of "her" strategy.

In fact, her attempts to restructure the organization to support the execution of "her" strategy were also unpopular. Staff members were expected to respond to three bosses: one from each business, function, and region. The reorganization also involved combining the entire organization into two front-end sales and marketing organizations, and two back-end research and development and manufacturing organizations.

Among her most visible and extreme actions was the merging of HP with Compaq to create a large, low-cost supplier of personal computers and servers. The merger became a hot bed of discussion in the press, among staff members and in the HP boardroom. Fiorina fought hard for the merger and won. When the dust settled, she did manage to show cost savings by eliminating redundant personnel. But her execution of the merger and the shift to becoming a low-cost commodity supplier failed. She did not deliver enough of her promise to HP's Board and shareholders.

Eventually, resistance to the Compaq-HP merger and to a leadership style so contradictory to the HP Way forced Fiorina to resign in 2005.

Mark Hurd joined HP in early 2005. He'd spent 25 years at NCR as CEO and president. Hurd was named chairman of HP's Board of Directors in September 2006—a selection that marked a return to the HP Way.

Hurd won the Board over by walking into his first meeting with them and articulating what he saw as the problem and how he would resolve it.

When Hurd joined HP, he did not make any fundamental changes to the strategy. In fact, many of his initial actions were in exact contrast to his predecessor's. While Fiorina immediately started acting, Hurd determined what the right actions were. He spent much time connecting with people across all businesses and testing the beliefs he had presented to the Board.

Less flamboyant than Fiorina, Hurd spoke honestly about the challenges HP faced. He focused on the need for everyone to work together—values similar to its founders and the time-honored HP Way.

Hurd used his first hundred days to analyze the situation by meeting staff members and customers.

In this period, he met over a thousand customers. Hurd's perspective was that the vision would come after he used his first hundred days to understand the current status of the organization. In hindsight, Hurd did benefit from the work of his predecessor; he did not need to look at the vision because it was already in place.

But where Fiorina had focused on the big picture, Hurd managed the detail. When Hurd asked his managers for plans, he expected them to set reachable goals and hold people accountable. He is known for this attention to detail. In a well-received first step, he terminated the joint agreement with HP and Apple iPod.

Many experts recommended at the time he took over that HP break off its highly profitable printer business. They expected it to be one of Hurd's first major actions. Instead, he broke up the two units (which his predecessor had combined) to make them more accountable. Hurd also started aggressive cost-cutting measures that eliminated most outside consultants and gradually cut the workforce by 10 percent. He also reversed Friona's organization redesign and went back to giving his managers more autonomy.

Within three years, Hurd had reinstated the HP Way and revitalized HP itself. By paying attention to the culture and leveraging the HP Way to implement strategy, he succeeded where Fiorina failed. What kind of success did he achieve? In August 2006, HP far surpassed Dell in PC sales growth and had matched its profitability.

The outside world applauded this strong leader. In 2008, Hurd was voted the number one executive in the U.S. in Channel Web's "Top 25 Executives of 2008."

Channel Web's Web site stated its reason for giving Hurd the award:

> In an industry full of hype and hot air, Hurd is the real deal. He focuses squarely day in and day out on making improvements in the business that either take costs out or drive sales. He's the ultimate operations-oriented CEO. And he gets the channel, every nook and cranny of it. Not just the view from the ivory tower, but also the rough and tumble goings on in the sales trenches.
>
> He's not about ego and image. He's all about results. What a refreshing change after the ever-image-conscious Carly Fiorina.[4]

The March 2009 issue of *Fortune* contained an article called "Mark Hurd's Moment." The article commented on how Hurd rises at 4:45 every morning, without an alarm clock, so as not to be caught out by a competitor on a different time zone. It goes on to credit his success to his "mantra of efficiency" and his numbers.[5]

Vision without execution is nothing. Whenever anyone asks me about vision, I get very nervous. You've got to be able to tie it back to strategy; you've got to tie accountability to things.

—Mark Hurd, CEO of HP

Abandon Yesterday

The final message in this chapter is that you must abandon yesterday. You can no longer assume that what was successful for you yesterday will achieve the same success for you tomorrow. Organizations must be prepared to change much more frequently than they have ever been required to do in the past.

Today, both product and organizational life cycles are becoming shorter and shorter. For example, Microsoft's operating system, XP, has the shortest product life cycle of all its operating systems. The speed at which we operate today has resulted in strategies lasting for shorter periods, and as a result leaders need to craft strategy more frequently. This naturally means that they need to implement the strategy more frequently, and so it places an even greater emphasis on the need to be excellent at execution. Only a decade ago, we used to develop a strategy and it would last over five years. Today, you are lucky if the strategy lasts three years.

You must abandon yesterday much more quickly than you have ever done before. We can no longer plan the future as an extension of yesterday. Consider that in 1985, according to Standard and Poor's, 35 percent of organizations were regarded as high risk, 24 percent average, and 41 percent low risk. Twenty-one years later, 14 percent were regarded as low risk, 14 percent were average, and 73 percent were high risk! Economists call this a "secular shift"—a broad increase in uncertainty and volatility. It reflects the challenge of businesses to deliver long-term sustainable earnings growth.

As the late Peter Drucker observed, "Maintaining yesterday is difficult and time-consuming and therefore always commits the institution's scarcest and most valuable resources—and above all, its ablest people—to non-results."[6] Which means such organizations are not available to create tomorrow.

The speed of change today places even more emphasis on being able to execute strategy by doing it right the first time. Leaders must sharpen their tools and be more agile, observant, and flexible than they have ever had to be in the past. The story of Google in the sidebar is a case in point.

Google

Google thrives on chaos and has a culture that responds to rapid change. Often voted as the best place to work in the United States, it has a unique culture. In September 1998, Google Inc. opened its door in Menlo Park, California. The door came with a remote control, as it was attached to the garage. The office offered several big advantages, including a washer and dryer, and a hot tub. It also provided a parking space for the first employee hired by the new organization: Craig Silverstein, now Google's director of technology.

Today, "Googleplex" headquarters is crammed with conference rooms, hallway buzz sessions, sandy volleyball courts, youngsters whizzing around on motorized scooters, and an "anything goes" spirit. It has 17 cafes that span 20 cuisines and are legendary for their fantastic food. Engineers spend 20 percent of their time pursuing their own ideas. The hierarchy is flat, and when Sheryl Sandberg, a former VP, made a mistake that cost it several million dollars, she walked across the street to inform Larry Page (the co-founder). His reply, "I'm so glad you made this mistake." Why, because if Google was not taking risks, then it would not keep evolving.

The challenge for any leader today is to recognize the rapid rate at which strategies need to change and respond accordingly.

Summary—Leaders' Role in Implementation

Two things leaders must do differently:

1. **Understand the organization's culture.**
   Leaders have a responsibility to review the culture of the organization and to make sure it supports the strategy and drives their unique implementation.

   The CEO's ultimate goal is to develop a culture that is self-reinforcing toward implementing the strategy. Culture does not drive strategy, it drives the way you implement the strategy.

   Changing the Culture element, however, is the hardest challenge of all the points on the Implementation Compass and requires tremendous time, effort, and focus from the leaders. Organizations that embark on a culture-changing program have a very tough challenge ahead of them.

   The HP case study illustrates just how important it is to ensure culture drives your implementation. Where Fiorina failed was to recognize the strong internal values and culture of HP and their relationship to her strategy. Hurd, in contrast, leveraged the HP Way to successfully implement the strategy.

2. **Abandon yesterday.**
   The life of a strategy is becoming shorter and shorter, and as a result we can no longer assume that what worked yesterday

will work tomorrow. Also, as we need to create new strategies more frequently, leaders need to implement more frequently, and as a result there has never been a greater need to be excellent in execution.

The speed of change today places even more emphasis on being able to execute strategy by doing it right the first time. Leaders must sharpen their tools and be more agile, observant, and flexible than they have ever had to be in the past.

Endnotes

1 G. Moore, *Crossing the Chasm* (New York: HarperCollins, 2002).
2 Zappos.com. "Zappos Core Values," 1999–2009; accessed at http://about.zappos.com/our-unique-culture/zappos-core-values, June 3, 2009.
3 Dave Packard, *The HP Way: How Bill Hewlett and I Built Our Company* (New York: HarperCollins, 1995).
4 "The Top 25 Executives of 2008," ChannelWeb, n.d.; accessed at www.crn.com/it-channel/212101428;jsessionid=W1RSCZWURHA0CQSNDLRCKHSCJUNN2JVN?pgno=2, June 3, 2009.
5 Adam Lashinsky, "Mark Hurd's Moment," *Fortune* magazine. March 3, 2009, accessed at http://money.cnn.com/2009/02/27/news/companies/lashinsky_hurd.fortune/index.htm, June 3, 2009.
6 e-BIM Editorial Staff, "Abandoning the Obsolete and Unproductive: A Difficult but Necessary Task." November 17, 2008; accessed at www.sixsigmaiq.com/Columnarticle.cfm?externalID=387&ColumnID=11, June 3, 2009.

8

PROCESS

A lousy process will consume 10 times as many hours as the work itself requires. A good process will eliminate the wasted time.

—Bill Gates, CEO of Microsoft

Obsolete yourself or the competition will.
—Lew Platt, former CEO of Hewlett-Packard

One of the key reasons why even great strategies fail to be implemented is that processes and or systems have not been changed to support the new strategy, and as a result staff members are working the old way, using old systems, structures, and processes, and they are expected to deliver different results!

When implementing a new strategy leaders have to step back and ask, "Do our processes support or hinder the new way of working?" In many organizations, they hinder the desired behaviors and actions required to execute the new strategy. Staff members are asked to work with processes that are more troublesome than helpful and systems that are too slow, and they spend too much time doing work that is not even value-adding to the old strategy, never mind the new one! In this chapter, I examine how to ensure the organization's support for the new way of working. I also discuss ways to redesign processes based on the latest thinking. Process redesign has the potential to dramatically improve the bottom line as well as drive the implementation.

Non-Value-Adding

It is estimated that one-third of a typical process is non-value-adding in medium-sized and large organizations. In other words, staff members are doing work that does not add any value for the customer, business, or shareholder. They are wasting a third of every day fixing past mistakes or checking work when there is no requirement or redoing work that was not done right the first time. The implementation of the new strategy provides an excellent opportunity to redesign processes and to eliminate non-value-adding work. This can lead to a dramatic improvement in bottom-line revenue and engage staff members in the implementation, as process redesign is at the heart of what they do every day.

The redesign of a process has a direct impact on the people responsible for implementing the strategy—the staff members—and also provides them an opportunity to understand what they need to do differently. In addition, the redesign of processes also has a major impact on customer satisfaction, employee satisfaction, reducing defects and cycle time, and, most importantly, revenue.

In the last few years, after a plethora of process redesign approaches, we are finally becoming better at it. Six Sigma has been a frontrunner for the last few years and contains best practices that have evolved from previous efforts. I do not advocate adopting Six Sigma in all cases, as its usefulness depends on the objectives of your strategy. I do, however, advocate adopting some of its best practices.

Figure 8.1 illustrates the evolution of key process redesign methodologies starting from the 1900s. It is not all inclusive, but it does show

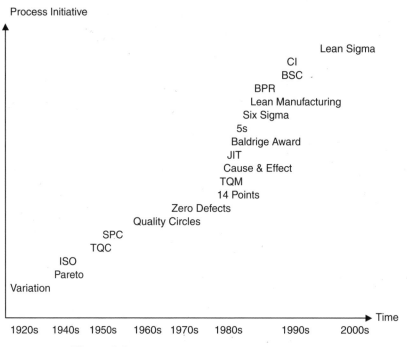

Process Initiative

Lean Sigma
CI
BSC
BPR
Lean Manufacturing
Six Sigma
5s
Baldrige Award
JIT
Cause & Effect
TQM
14 Points
Zero Defects
Quality Circles
SPC
TQC
ISO
Pareto
Variation

1920s   1940s   1950s   1960s 1970s   1980s   1990s   2000s   Time

Figure 8.1   Key Process Redesign Methodologies.

how process redesign is still a relatively new methodology in business today. Some of the dates may surprise you on just how long the methodology has been around.

Methodology	Description
Variation	Dr. Walter Shewhart of the Bell Laboratories (U.S.) first made the distinction between "controlled" and "uncontrolled" variation in work processes.
Pareto	Juran discovered the work of Vilfredo Pareto and popularized the 80/20 Rule.
ISO (International Organization for Standardization)	Includes ISO 9001, which became popular in the 1980s.
TQC (Total Quality Control)	Focuses on examining the processes in an operation to identify and rectify mistakes.

Methodology	Description
SPC (Statistical Processing Control)	An effective method of monitoring a process through the use of control charts that continued to grow in popularity throughout the 1900s.
Quality circles	First established in Japan in 1962 and credited to Kaoru Ishikawa.
Zero Defects	Philip Crosby's principle of "doing it right the first time" (DIRFT).
14 Points	Deming's 14 Points for management; it popularizes Shewhart's Plan: Do—Check—Act Cycle.
TQM (Total Quality Management)	"Total," because it is concerned with all work processes and the way they can be improved to better meet customer needs.
Cause & Effect	The Ishikawa diagram or Fish Bone diagram to identify root causes.
JIT (Just-in-time)	An inventory strategy implemented to improve the return on investment of a business by reducing in-process inventory and its associated carrying costs.
Baldrige Award	Malcolm Baldrige National Quality Award introduced by the U.S. government to encourage business excellence.
5s	A mnemonic for a program focused on having visual order, organization, cleanliness, and standardization.
Six Sigma	A business management strategy, originally developed by Motorola, introduced the Define, Measure, Analyze, Improve, and Control process (along with GE).
Lean manufacturing	Strives to reduce waste of any type and is based on the Toyota production system.
BPR	Michael Hammer's business process reengineering.

Methodology	Description
CI (Continuous Improvement)	Focuses on improving customer satisfaction through continuous and incremental improvements to processes.
BSC (Balanced Scorecard)	A performance management approach that focuses on various overall performance indicators.
Lean Sigma	A special sequence that is claimed to deliver higher results than if each one of the continuous methodologies were used individually.

Three Best Practices to Adopt

From Six Sigma and the other process redesign approaches, I have identified three best practices that I recommend adopting when redesigning processes in the organization.

- Focus on revenue generated.
- Use Strategic Process Redesign (SPR).
- Focus on the customer (both internal and external).

Focus on Revenue Generated from Redesigned Processes

When implementing your strategy, you have to change the way your staff members work. A new strategy means doing things differently, and process redesign is the catalyst for changing processes to support the strategy and also to improve profitability. Many organizations have even adopted Six Sigma as their strategy to create competitive advantage. However, it is important to note that some experts, including Tom Peters and Michael Porter, argue that process improvement does not create a strategic advantage as the competition can easily copy the differences.

It is also important to note that process redesign is not about improving cycle times and reducing defects. It is about generating additional revenue. Improving cycle times and reducing defects are the by-products of process improvement.

There is another school of thought that says Six Sigma is a culture change and is a strategic advantage, which is why Motorola, General Electric, and Citigroup CEOs, for example, all chose to adopt it.

In the late 1990s, when John Reid was CEO of Citibank, he asked a number of top performers from over the 100 countries that Citibank operated in, to form teams and identify how Citibank could distance itself from its competitors. The bank was already number one and Reid wanted to ensure not only that it remained number one but also that the gap widened from the banks competitors. Various approaches and best practices were examined in other organizations. In the end, Reid decided to adopt Six Sigma and behavioral change. A large part of the reason was that when processes were improved, it allowed the staff members to make the changes and thus everyone in the Bank could play a part in implementing the strategy. Twelve months after launching the initiative globally, the bank reported to the analysts a conservative increase of US$500,000 million directly to the bottom line.

Within 24 months, Reid entered into a merger with Sandy Weill, and Six Sigma mostly ended up in the corporate graveyard of failed strategies. There were, however, a few countries that continued to use the Six Sigma approach largely due to the fact the chief country officer (CCO, the CEO equivalent) had seen the financial benefits. Despite not only the merger but the financial crises, terrorism, and the bubble bursting, many of the CCOs in the Asia-Pacific region continued to practice Six Sigma. Each year, the revenue gains dramatically increased.

One early example within Citibank came from the redesign of the foreign exchange (FX) process. GE Capital, which was also adopting Six Sigma, pulled together the 17 banks in Singapore it did business with and explained that in future, if an FX transaction was not completed within one hour, then GE Capital would no longer give that bank its FX business. It then handed out envelopes with each bank's rating against the other banks. Citibank was number one—and it still took four hours to complete the average FX transaction.

The treasury team adopted Six Sigma methodology to redesign the process. Within four months, a new process was implemented and GE Capital FX transactions were completed within 55 minutes. Although GE only said that it would stop conducting business "if you couldn't complete the FX in less than one hour," Citibank saw an increase in FX volume as it was the fastest to respond and the only bank at the time able to complete the transaction in less than one hour. As a result of reducing defects and improving cycle times, the leaders saw a dramatic increase in profitability.

One of the key reasons Six Sigma has been successful is that it shows you the revenue generated. A redesign project returns on average US$250,000 from both cost savings and newly generated revenue.

Previous quality initiatives did not show the revenue benefits. Using the principles of Six Sigma, every project tracks the financial impact.

To calculate the financial benefits from any process redesign, you need to ask three questions:

- *What is the current revenue generated from the process?* This will provide baseline data that show where you currently are.
- *What is the estimated financial impact of the project?* Consider both the cost savings and the potential revenue.
- *What is the market potential?* Consider the larger picture.

When answering these questions, spell out any assumptions you have made, such as the competition not introducing a new product, interest rates staying the same, or customer demand surging.

This is an important step, as stating the assumptions up front can avoid many of the discussions and arguments that can consume a meeting on the primary source of increased revenue.

LEADER'S ROLE IN PROCESS REDESIGN Many staff members welcome the opportunity to improve processes they have to suffer with every day. A leader's role is twofold. First, provide the opportunity to make improvements, and second, champion at least one of the projects to show support for the staff members' initiative. I will discuss how to provide staff members the opportunity to make improvements in the next section, "Strategic Process Redesign."

As champion of a project redesign, the leader needs to liaise with the head of the project team, provide guidance and motivation when necessary, and oversee the team's success. The role is designed to minimize interruptions in responsibilities while maximizing benefits to a team.

Key responsibilities include:

- Mentor the team to successful completion.
- Attend the first and last meeting.
- Provide support and guidance throughout the project.
- Remove roadblocks when required.
- Liaise with the team leader.

Process redesign not only provides staff members an opportunity to participate in the implementation by redesigning the work flow, but also an opportunity to add substantially to the bottom line.

Strategic Process Redesign

When considering how to improve a process, various methodologies are available. Bridges has consolidated the best practices into a methodology that generates the greatest revenue benefits while redesigning the processes. We call it Strategic Process Redesign (SPR).

SPR adopts lessons learned from previous failures and successes of redesign methodologies, including Six Sigma and other process redesign initiatives. It combines both process redesign and project management, and it sets a team up for success.

When an organization has decided to redesign its processes the leadership is faced with the challenge of identifying the best way to do it. This question can consume the leaders and even end up in stalling the process redesign if the team can't agree. SPR is a structured and detailed approach that breaks down what needs to happen. It offers the following advantages:

- A structured and tested approach
- Process redesign combined with project management
- Processes aligned to the new strategy
- Best practices from previous initiatives
- A customer-centric approach
- Focus on delivering revenue

At the heart of SPR is cross-functional process mapping, which is an approach that has been tremendously successful globally. It tasks a team to look at a process from end to end, not just within a silo. That means following the product or service from the customer to every department or function that touches the process and back to the customer. Cross-functional process mapping involves five stages:

1. *Planning*—takes two weeks and is done in the office.
2. *Current stage mapping*—a three-day offsite to identify issues.
3. *Validation*—other staff members review the map and issues.
4. *Desired stage mapping*—a three-day offsite to redesign and identify actions.
5. *Implementation and harvest*—12 weeks to implement and track benefits.

FIVE STAGES OF CROSS-FUNCTIONAL PROCESS MAPPING The advantage of adopting SPR and using cross-functional process mapping is that it creates both quantum and incremental results, and preempts many of the typical questions practitioners ask, such as, "Why map the current state when everyone knows the problems?" (The answer is that it allows staff members to identify the issues and baseline data, and also ensures that all the team members understand the process end-to-end.) Without the methodology, teams typically waste time arguing approaches and methodologies rather than moving ahead with the process redesign.

The five stages of cross-functional process mapping have been tested and have a purpose. For example, very few people have looked at a process end to end and know all the issues. A typical current state map will wind up listing more than 250 issues. The number of issues surprises most teams and leaders. In addition, by mapping out the current state, the baseline is identified and therefore the improvement can be measured.

During the desired stage redesign process, in cross-functional process mapping, no investment is made in people or technology. For people, it is because it is easy for a boss to double the workforce and work twice as fast. For technology, it is because if you automate a process before you clean it up, then all you could be doing is providing bad service . . . faster. Only after the desired stage has been implemented are new systems or additional people considered. In addition, the large financial and non-financial benefits that come from this stage and these benefits can be used for any future investment.

The methodology involves looking at a process from end to end across many functions. It starts and ends with the customer. The term *function* is used instead of *department* as one department may have many functions.

A good project will:

- Solve a critical customer issue
- Reduce defects and cycle times
- Use quality tools for analysis of root causes and problem resolution
- Establish smart goals up front
- Create quantum improvements
- Quantify financial benefits

LEADERS' ROLE IN SPR The leaders' role does not include getting involved in process redesign. They do not know the work. In SPR it is the people who do the work who are invited to redesign the process. This is their task, not the leaders', as it is the staff members rather than the leaders who are the ones answering phones, meeting customers, and delivering goods and services.

The leaders' role is to assist in the early stages by selecting the right process and the right people to be involved. Once the process is selected the leaders then champion the process redesign. Once a few processes have been redesigned, the leaders can hand off the selection of both the process and people, as teams better understand what is required.

A global electronics organization was making its first foray into process redesign without learning from others' past experience. Its initial attempts failed due to two expensive mistakes. First, middle and senior managers were invited to do the redesign, and although they had done the work 5 or 10 years earlier, they now only oversaw the process and did not know the detailed current work process. Second, the process adopted was too large. A global process was selected, and although the redesign would benefit customers the implementation failed as it involved too many people in too many countries. In hindsight the organization learned the hard way that it had the wrong people involved and too large a scope.

SPR guides leaders in what works and what to avoid so as not to repeat the mistakes of the past and to provide every opportunity of success. A best practice within SPR is that the staff members selected for the redesign must be top performers.

When selecting a process redesign, the decision alone can take many months. Some leaders adopt the GE "Work-Out," use simple brainstorming, or even worse—they just tell a team to do it, without providing any guidance. On many of these occasions the teams fail or make very minor changes. SPR provides the structure and creates quantum and incremental results. Like any approach, however, SPR has both advantages and disadvantages.

Disadvantages of SPR

- It takes three months to simply redesign the process and another three months to implement the changes.
- It involves pulling out your best people from their day-to-day activities and it is time-consuming.
- It may be expensive to hire facilitators to guide you through if you do not have the internal resources.
- The approach may be more than is required.

Advantages of SPR

- It generates an average profit of US$250,000 per project.
- It creates quantum and incremental improvements; for example, working 10 times faster.
- Is a structured, well-tested approach.
- It avoids long discussions and arguments among leaders and team members trying to agree on the best approach.
- It combines both process excellence and project management.
- It is customer-centric.
- It works.

As champion, a leader's role does not end when the team creates the redesign. It is critical that leaders also focus on supporting the implementation of the actions created in the desired stage. It is in the implementation of the actions that most projects fail.

Focus on the Customer (Internal and External)

"The customer is king." This is a statement that has led to many a downfall among customer service initiatives and process redesign projects.

In their enthusiasm to become customer-centric, many organizations allowed the pendulum to swing too far and adopted a blinkered approach, maintaining that customers could do no wrong; they were king. But customers lie, customers are rude, and customers cheat. The customer is not king. The correct positioning is that the customer is always important. It is how we deal with different customers that is important, as the story "The Customer's Place" reflects.

The Customer's Place

When Herb Keller was CEO of Southwest Airlines, the marketing department received a four-page letter from a customer complaining about boarding, the seats, the cabin crew, and many more things. The marketing team worked on the reply for three days and then checked with Herb before sending the reply. Herb read the customer letter and the marketing reply. He tore up the marketing reply and wrote on the customer letter, "Southwest is not for you, please enjoy flying on the other airlines." The reason was simple: this customer did not have the right profile for the airline and the CEO immediately recognized this and did not want his team spending time on the wrong customer segment.

When redesigning a process, make sure it starts and ends with external customers, and take the time to clearly understand their needs and expectations. In the redesign, however, the customer requirements should not be blindly followed. They must be weighed against the process redesign goal. After all, if we always listened to the customer then we would never have 24-hour news; as it was, customers who said it was not required.

The objective of focusing on customers is to redesign the process around them so that you ensure changes are value-adding and not just for change's sake. On many occasions, proposed changes have been more internally focused and been of no benefit to the end user, or worse, even detrimental to the customer. As the German proverb says, "Change and change for the better are two different things."

To ensure that the changes add value for the customers, leaders must clearly know their customers' expectation. This can be achieved by increasing the number of listening posts between the organization and its customers.

Traditional listening posts have included surveys, focus groups, interviews, formalized complaint systems, market research, and mystery shopper programs. Today we are also using targeted and multi-level interviews and surveys, customer scorecards, data warehousing and data mining, and customer and supplier audits. The end result is that we should not rely on a once-a-year customer survey; instead, we should identify critical processes from the customers' perspectives and then ensure we know their expectations and track them at least quarterly.

For example, one of the banks I worked with started its process redesign by first identifying the critical processes across the bank as the starting point. It identified seven critical processes and ensured that they had multiple listening posts for each:

- Account opening
- Credit decision and solution delivery
- Transaction delivery
- Statements and integrated customer information

- Inquiry investigation
- Access availability
- Customer wait time

Once the bank identified the critical processes, it then put in place measures to track performance and when necessary redesigned processes. This had a positive impact upstream on the drivers of customer satisfaction and revenue.

In another example, I worked on a process redesign in Vietnam, a salesman explained that customers had to complete a particular form in triplicate before the organization could do business with them. It was the law. Every salesman, when bringing on board a new customer, would have the customer fill in the form, in triplicate. Fortunately, we had a lawyer in the room who commented it was not the law. The salesman strongly and passionately defended the form. The lawyer simply stated that it was not the law.

The form filling had become so entrenched as part of the process of introducing a new customer that the salesman could not comprehend that it was not a legal requirement. The value of the cross-functional mapping was that many non-value-adding steps were eliminated. This type of discussion is not unusual, as people from different functions come together and map the process end-to-end for the first time. The most common expression I hear is, "I never knew that you do that."

The facilitator's role (black or green belt, to use Six Sigma terms) is to ensure that the changes made add value to the internal or external customer, or both. One methodology for identifying disconnects or issues in an organization is to hold weekly disconnect meetings.

WEEKLY DISCONNECT MEETINGS Another powerful best practice is to initiate weekly disconnect meetings between sales and operations to discuss issues. Whether it is the waiters and chefs, front office and back office, or sales and operations, the objective is to voice, track, and improve issues that disrupt the business.

The cooperation and communication between the front and the back office can be a cornerstone of SPR. In weekly disconnect meetings, representatives meet from front and back-office functions to discuss daily disconnects and business issues. During the week, functions track and record disconnects as they happen in the business and then present the disconnects at the meeting. It is important to note that these meetings focus on the disconnects and not the people. At no time should this become a finger-pointing exercise. If it does, the approach will fail.

At the start of the meeting, which lasts no more than 90 minutes, the issues from the previous week are discussed first to ensure they have been resolved. Then new issues are discussed with the objective of eliminating them. If an issue requires more than a discussion or brief brainstorming session to be resolved, then it can be considered for process redesign.

THE DEVIL IS IN THE DETAIL The weekly disconnect meetings, when put into practice, allow organizations to focus on daily issues and the small details that otherwise are lost in the rush to complete the day-to-day business. When implementing strategy the devil is in the detail. It is taking care of the small things that makes a large difference. Here lies the paradox. Strategy is the "big think"; implementation is about managing the detail.

To successfully implement strategy, leaders must move from looking at the macro perspective to the micro, while keeping an eye on the macro. They can't become too focused on the big picture or on the small details. They must find the right balance.

Porsche CEO Wendelin Wiedeking is known throughout the organization for his attention to detail, and that is the part of his leadership style that has helped Porsche thrive while so many of its competitors are struggling to stay alive.

Here are a few amusing examples of what happens when you do not focus on the details:

- In December 2005, a Japanese share dealer tried to sell one share in a recruitment organization for 600,000 yen (US$6,000), but accidentally sold 600,000 shares at one yen. His mistake landed his organization with a bill for US$250 million.
- A slip of the finger by a clerk led Bear Stearns, the investment bank, to erroneously enter an order to sell £2.3 billion of stocks. The bank managed to cancel all but £350 million of the orders.
- Scientists working on the Mars Climate Orbiter, a US$140 million spacecraft, mixed up their imperial and metric measurements, causing it to burn up in the red planet's atmosphere.

When you start to take care of the small things, customers start to notice. They do not notice immediately, as there is a time lag before internal process improvements have an impact on the external customer. This is also why there is not an immediate improvement in customer satisfaction; it can take up to six months before you see a positive impact. Another reason why customer satisfaction does not improve in the initial few months of redesigning a process is that the first time the organization does it right, the customer thinks it is a fluke! For years, the organization has been screwing things up and suddenly, it gets it right. The customer only starts to believe in improvement when it happens repeatedly.

Summary—Leaders' Role in Implementation

Two things leaders must do differently:

1. **Make sure processes support the new strategy's objectives.**
   Leaders must take a long, hard look at the current way the organization works and ask what processes need to change to support staff members' ability to execute the strategy.

2. **Adopt best practices from previous quality initiatives.**
   When improving a process, the best approach is to learn from previous redesign efforts and adopt a methodology that will work in the organization culture. The three best practices to adopt from previous initiatives:

   - Focus on revenue generated
     Process redesign creates exceptional opportunity to improve bottom-line revenue and engage staff members in the implementation, as process redesign is at the heart of what they do every day. It is not about improving cycle times and reducing defects. It is about improving the bottom line. Improving cycle times and reducing defects are the by-products of process improvement.
     Many staff members welcome the opportunity to improve the obsolete processes they have to use every day. The leader's role is threefold. First, provide staff members the opportunity to make improvements, champion at least one of the projects to show their support, and ensure that every project tracks the financial benefits.

   - Strategic Process Redesign (SPR)
     Strategic Process Redesign (SPR) is a Bridges approach, adopting lessons learned from previous failures and successes, best practices from Six Sigma and other process

redesign methodologies. It combines both process redesign and project management, and it guides a team to success.

The advantage of adopting SPR and using cross-functional process mapping, which is at the heart of SPR, is that it creates both quantum and incremental results, and in addition it preempts many of the typical questions that arise during a redesign. This assists in avoiding time-wasting discussions of the best way to do things, and it allows the organization to keep moving forward.

When adopting SPR, leaders do not get involved in the process redesign, as they do not know the work. In SPR, it is the people who do the work who are invited to redesign the process—in other words, the staff members.

The leaders' role is to assist in the early stages in selecting the right process and to ensure the right people are involved—the mavericks. Leaders must also champion a process redesign to demonstrate their commitment. After the first few redesigns, leaders can hand off the selection of both the process and people, as teams will have started to understand what is required.

Leaders must also support the implementation of the actions in the process redesign. This (just like strategy implementation) is where most redesigns falter, as it is the biggest challenge.

- Focus on customers (both internal and external)

    The redesign of a process is customer-centric. To ensure that the changes add value for the customers, it is often important to increase the number of listening posts between the organization and its customers.

    Improvements to the process must benefit customers. Many organizations still slip back to making improvements that benefit themselves internally, but not external customers.

    Leaders must also manage the small details to make significant improvements. Weekly disconnect meetings should be held to allow organizations to focus on daily issues and the small details that otherwise are lost in the rush to complete the day-to-day business. When implementing strategy, the devil is in the detail. The cooperation and communication between the front and the back office can be a cornerstone to SPR.

9

REINFORCE

A leader is best when people barely know he exists
Not so good when people obey and acclaim him
Worst of all when they despise him
Fail to honor people and they fail to honor you
But a good leader, who talks little
When his work is done, his aim fulfilled
They will say, we did this ourselves.

—Lao-Tzu

Unless staff members have realistic incentives to implement the
strategy, they will not commit to it and the implementation will
fail. The leader's goal under Reinforce is to ensure that the right

actions and behaviors are being encouraged through recognition and reward. Just as what gets measured gets done, the same philosophy can be applied to reinforcement. The right reinforcement drives the right actions and behaviors.

Organizations that do not provide the right rewards and opportunities wind up training their talent for their competition.

—Scott Cohen, talent management expert

Leaders must reinforce the behaviors and actions they want to see. Many organizations change their strategy but not the way they reinforce desired performance. As a result, their staff members do not change the behaviors or actions they are taking. Even if leaders have changed the measurement system and have the right KPIs in place, the implementation will most likely fail if they have not aligned the reinforcement with the strategy outcomes.

In this chapter, I discuss the importance of aligning the Rewards and Recognition, Competencies, Measures, and the "Employee Engagement Cycle."

The impact of reinforcement can be accentuated through an example from leadership expert David Cottrell, who recalls an organization that was growing quickly, but couldn't keep up in production. In particular, it was having trouble ensuring that orders would be shipped by 5 PM on the day they were received. Completion time was stretching toward 7 PM, and as a result overtime costs were increasing.

Following an employee's suggestion, management extended the work shift hours to 7 PM and started paying employees at their regular pay rate for those evening hours. If employees finished the orders earlier, however, they were allowed to go home—and still get paid for the balance of the time left on the shift. Before long all orders were being done by the original 5 PM deadline. The opportunity to earn more without staying longer called forth untapped energy and creativity.

Task Force 1—Reward and Recognition Review

Forget praise.
Forget punishment.
Forget cash.
You need to make their jobs more interesting.

—Frederick Herzberg, industrial psychologist

I define *rewards* as staff members' pay—or rice bowl (as we say in Asia), and *recognition* as nonfinancial rewards. The leader's challenge is to oversee the review of both the organization's rewards and recognitions. This is the most sensitive area of the eight directions on the compass. One wrong move can be the downfall of the implementation, which is why it is imperative that leaders oversee the changes.

A task force should be initiated to review the alignment of the current rewards and recognition against the objectives of the new strategy. The task force is a combination of HR and line managers. It should not just be made up of HR representatives, as you need a more balanced perspective. As with a process redesign team, the task force should also have a steering committee made up from the leaders.

The task force begins by reviewing the current rewards and recognition against the new desired behaviors and actions required to execute the new strategy.

These are the three fundamental questions the task force discusses:

- What actions and behaviors do staff members need to adopt to execute the strategy objectives?
- What actions and behaviors do the current rewards and reinforcement encourage?
- What needs to change in the way we reward and recognize out staff members?

Depending on the size of the organization, the task force should be able to submit its recommendations to the steering committee within 90 days.

On completion of the review, the task force presents its recommendations to the steering committee for consideration. The implementation of the recommendations is then delegated to the leader responsible for the area.

---

61 percent of U.S. workers say they received no meaningful rewards or recognition for their efforts last year. 71 percent of workers consider themselves disengaged—clock-watchers who can't wait to go home.

—Wall Street Journal/*Gallup Poll*

An Essential Element

It is essential to have alignment between the new behaviors and actions and the way staff members are rewarded and recognized. For example, when FedEx wanted to be more customer-centric, it introduced a Customer Satisfaction Index (CSI). After 12 months, however, it became clear that leaders were not reacting to the results. To overcome this, it linked 33 percent of leaders' bonuses to the CSI. This got leaders' attention and drove the desired actions and behaviors.

When Lou Gerstner took over as CEO of IBM, he saw signs everywhere promoting teamwork, but when he checked how staff members were paid, he discovered that it was based on individual performance. Adjusting the IBM reward system to support group effort became a high priority for him.

Simultaneously, you must also encourage the desired actions and behaviors through additional reinforcement. When GE rolled out Six Sigma, it wanted to encourage staff members to participate, a challenge every organization faces. The approach adopted by GE was unusually powerful, demonstrating to staff members how serious the leadership team was about the new strategy. The team made it mandatory that to be promoted, staff members had to be certified in "Green Belt" training—Six Sigma facilitation and process training. It also told staff members that any who became "Black Belts" were guaranteed promotion after two years. The logic was very straightforward. Staff members who had been Black Belts for two years had been trained in the skills of Six Sigma, had demonstrated leadership attributes, and had had exposure to different businesses and the way they worked. It was a win–win situation that successfully encouraged the actions and behaviors GE wanted from its staff members.

Avoid Cash as a Motivator (in Developed Economies)

When you examine ways to improve recognition in your organization, I strongly recommend this guideline: don't use cash. This is because cash is not a motivator in a developed economy, it is a demotivator.

For instance, when staff members have a comfortable lifestyle—for example, they have a good home, their kids have the latest MP3 player, and the latest 42-inch flat screen TV is sitting in the living room—a few extra dollars do not motivate them over the long term to take the right actions or demonstrate the right behaviors (they have satisfied the basic levels on Maslow's hierarchy of needs). In a developed economy, money diminishes as a motivator and is ranked in many surveys at number five.

Believe it or not, the number one motivator of staff members in a developed economy is two words: *thank you*. This is because staff members want to feel they are contributing to something greater than they could achieve on their own, and when their boss says "thank you" this is being accomplished.

A few extra dollars will not make a significant difference to them. Also, when you give them cash, they will most likely put it in their purse or wallet and forget what they spent it on. Or even worse, they might feel that you have assigned too small a value to the additional work they have done and see it as an insult.

Another occasion when money is a demotivator is when staff members work hard and they feel they are not paid enough for their effort. When they are paid enough, ironically, money is not a motivator.

In a study of 1,500 employees conducted by Dr, Gerald Graham, professor of management at Wichita State University, personal congratulations—by managers of employees who do a good job—was ranked first from 67 potential incentives he evaluated. Second was a personal note for good performance written by the manager.[1]

In a semi- or undeveloped economy, money is the number one motivator. If staff members who have not yet satisfied their basic needs work hard on an implementation project and after six months you turn round and say "thank you," they will also say two words back … and the second is still … "you"!

We know from 200 years of research that behavior is shaped by consequences.

If you recognize and reward behavior, it will tend to be repeated. If you ignore and punish behavior it will tend to stop. In short, you get what you reward. Although this is common sense, it is far from common practice.

—Bob Nelson, author and consultant

Task Force 2—Competency Management

In conjunction with the review of rewards and recognition, each staff member's competencies must also be examined. Changing strategy means leaders have a responsibility to ensure that their staff members have the right skills and knowledge to deliver the new strategy.

Competence management is an approach to align individual skills and knowledge with the overall strategic goals and objectives. The process allows an organization to develop its core and operational proficiencies, abilities, and expertise required to execute its strategy.

Competencies are skills and abilities—described in behavioral terms—that are teachable, observable, measurable, and critical to successful performance. They can be divided into two areas: personal and job factors.

Personal factors are the specific intrinsic characteristics required by the individuals to complete the work, and job factors are the skills required to perform the work.

The task force is the direct responsibility of the HR director, and it is optional to include anyone from outside the department. Working with the leader from each department, the task force identifies any additional competencies required for staff members. There is no need for a steering committee as individual leaders are the best people to review their staff members.

Reward and recognition are relatively constant across an organization. The competencies, however, are different for every department and possibly for every staff member. If the organization does not have the internal capabilities to conduct the review, the task forces can be outsourced to an HR consultancy.

If new competencies are required, the relevant training must be identified and provided to fill the competency gap. A significant benefit from this approach is that the training provided is targeted, relevant, and specific. On many occasions a new strategy is launched and an organization-wide training program is selected in conjunction. The program typically has mediocre results at best and within a few months, staff members return to the old way of doing things, as they receive no reinforcement after the training. Or worse, in some organizations, staff members' behavior deteriorates as they are shown what is potentially possible and then see the organization return to the way it was. This leaves staff members frustrated and dissatisfied.

Measurement Alignment

In Chapter 6, I discussed how measures drive behavior, and leaders need to make sure that the behaviors staff members are exhibiting actually support the new strategy. Staff members' behaviors and actions are driven by how they are measured and how they are rewarded and recognized.

If staff members are measured for performing a specific behavior or action but not rewarded or recognized for that behavior, will they still consistently perform that behavior or take the required action?

On most occasions, the answer is yes—they will, as the measure itself acts as a recognition, but for only for a short period of time. The issue is that the implementation of the strategy requires alignment of rewards and recognition, competencies, measures, and employee engagement. Only with full alignment between the four areas do the desired behaviors and actions become constant. The leader's role is to ensure the alignment and thus be providing support and encouragement to staff members to adopt and perform the behaviors and actions required to execute the strategy.

Leaders are responsible for ensuring that the KPIs from the Balanced Scorecard are aligned with rewards and recognition. This involves the owner of each KPI checking it against the recognition and making recommendations to the task force on rewards and recognition.

People do what they do because of what happens to them when they do it.

> —Aubrey Daniels, author and consultant

Employee Engagement Cycle

The final alignment is to the key activities in an employee's engagement. Each key activity must be reviewed and aligned to the new strategy. The employee engagement cycle identifies the key activities from hiring to reward and recognition.

Figure 9.1   Diagram of the Employee Engagement Cycle.

Activity	Action
Hiring and firing	With the launch of the new strategy, hiring should be reviewed to ensure that any new employees have the right attitude for executing the strategy. The skills and knowledge can be trained. Some employees may need to be let go if they hold the organization back from strategy execution (saboteurs).
Induction	Induction is an opportunity to positively influence new employees. The culture of the organization plays a large part in the design of the induction process. Do you want new employees to sit through a tedious first day of hearing and reading procedures, or to be inspired to perform their best?
Training	With a competency model in place, targeted, relevant, and specific training is provided to meet individual requirements.
Measure performance	Employees are encouraged to perform at their best by being measured against what is important.
Feedback	Employees are provided feedback on a regular basis on their performance (not annually). The most important person to provide the feedback is their immediate boss, as this is who they listen to the most.
Review	This is the employee's performance review, which should be conducted as an open review by the immediate boss at least twice a year.
Reward and recognition	Based on the review of the employee's competencies and performance (and not how well the boss likes the employee!), specific rewards and recognition are awarded.

Summary—Leaders' Role in Implementation

Four things leaders must do differently:

1. **Review rewards and recognition via a task force.**
   Staff members will adopt the required behaviors and actions to deliver the objectives for the new strategy only when it is

aligned with rewards and recognition, competencies, measures, and employee engagement.

Leaders need to initiate a task force to review the organization's financial rewards and nonfinancial recognition. The task force is a combination of HR and line managers. The three fundamental questions the task force discusses are:

- What actions and behaviors do the staff members need to adopt to achieve the strategy objectives?
- What actions and behaviors do the current rewards and reinforcement encourage?
- What needs to change?

The task force recommendations are presented to a steering committee. The actions selected by the steering committee are then delegated to the relevant leader.

If you are working in a developed economy, it is best not to try to use cash as a motivator.

2. **Review the organization's competencies.**
   A second task force should be initiated to review the organization's competencies in alignment with the requirements of the new strategy. Changing strategy means leaders have a responsibility to ensure that their staff members have the right skills and knowledge to deliver the new strategy.

   Competencies are the skills and abilities, described in behavioral terms, that are teachable, observable, measurable, and critical to successful performance. They can be divided into two areas: personal and job factors. Working with the leader from each department the task force will identify any additional competencies required for each staff member.

   A significant benefit from using a competency model is that the training provided is targeted, relevant, and specific.

3. **Align measures.**
   If staff members are measured for performing a specific behavior or action but not rewarded or recognized for the behavior or action, they will perform that behavior—but only for a short period of time.

   Implementation requires alignment of not just the measure but also the rewards and recognitions, competencies, and employee engagement. Only when there is full alignment do the new behaviors or actions become constant.

4. **Review the employee engagement cycle.**

The employee engagement cycle identifies the key activities from hiring and firing to reward and recognition. Each activity must be reviewed by an HR team to ensure that staff members are given every opportunity and the support to succeed.

The leader's role in reinforcement of the strategy is to ensure the provision of every support and encouragement to staff members to adopt and perform the behaviors and actions required to execute the new strategy.

Endnote

1 Bob Nelson, "No-cost Employee Recognition," ABA Marketing. September 1, 2002; accessed at www.allbusiness.com/management/3592826-1.html June 12, 2009.

10

REVIEW

He who smiles when something goes wrong, has someone to blame it on!

—Richard Nixon

However beautiful the strategy, you should occasionally look at the results.

—Sir Winston Churchill

The odds of successfully executing a strategy that isn't reviewed very frequently are slim to none. As you implement strategy, you move from the "big think" to the "doing." It is during the execution that it becomes clear that what sounded good in theory does not always work in practice. As a result, implementation must be reviewed to ensure we are achieving the desired strategic outcomes.

In many organizations, strategy and its implementation is reviewed only twice a year. This is neither frequent nor comprehensive enough. A leader delivers shareholder returns not only by crafting the right strategy but also by executing it. Leaders are paid to make things happen. It therefore naturally follows that they should frequently check to see how they are doing. Waiting six months to check on an implementation is a recipe for failure.

Those who cannot remember the past are condemned to repeat it.

—George Santayana, philosopher

In this chapter, I reflect on the importance of reviewing parts of the strategy implementation every two weeks, and the strategy in its entirety every three months, and on the contents of a strategy review. On the Implementation Compass, Review is the least practiced of the best practices among leaders.

Strategy Implementation Reviews

Strategy implementation should be reviewed in its entirety every quarter and every two weeks in small components. Every two weeks, a leadership team needs to meet to discuss different parts of the strategy so that within three months, they know how the whole strategy implementation is performing.

In the review, strategy must be the first item on the agenda. In the past, leadership teams have placed operational issues first on the agenda—and by the time they reached the strategy, they were usually running short on time, and rushed the discussion, or—worse—skipped it entirely. Most of us have been involved in meetings where too much time was spent on the first half of the agenda and not enough on the second.

A practice, by some leaders, is to separate strategy and operational meetings for 12–18 months after the launch. This allows leaders to stay focused on both areas and to apply the right amount of attention. The two meetings are then merged, as the disciplined focus becomes a common practice.

Strategy Implementation Reviews (SIRs) provide the platform and structure to ensure leaders constantly review execution. It is more than likely that during reviews, questions will arise about the strategy itself, but these should be set aside. When the strategy needs to be revisited, it should be held as a separate meeting. SIR meetings are not the platform for leaders to redesign strategy.

Sample of SIR Reviews

Review 1 — Review of strategy map, KPIs, and an update on actions.

Review 2 — Communication plan roll-out and its impact.

Review 3 — Evaluation of rewards and recognition, competency task forces, and an update on actions.

Review 4 — Actions update.

Review 5 — Update on process redesign.

Review 6 — Analysis of the culture alignment and a check on key actions.

When I suggest holding a leadership team meeting every two weeks to discuss strategy implementation, I'm usually met with raised eyebrows. Pause to consider, however, how often you have reviewed implementation during past efforts—and the success of the implementation. To change the horrendous failure rate of implementation, leaders must change their current attitudes and actions. Reviewing implementation every two weeks provides an excellent opportunity to improve the organizations chances of success and it also accomplishes a number of benefits:

1. It demonstrates the importance of the new strategy to the whole organization.
2. It changes the dialogue among leaders from talking mostly about operational issues to talking about strategic issues.
3. It assists in the cascade of the strategy through the organization.
4. It keeps the strategy on the leaders' radar.
5. It maintains leaders' focus on solving the strategic problems not the operational ones.

1. Demonstrate the Importance of the New Strategy

"Lead by example" is practically a cliché—but that doesn't make it less true. When the rest of the organization sees the leaders meeting every two weeks to discuss the strategy and its implementation, people know that management is serious. Likewise, when staff members see leaders meeting only twice a year on the strategy—they are likely to doubt the leadership's sincerity.

2. *Change the Dialogue*

Bridges research estimates that most leadership teams spend 85 percent of their time talking operationally and only 15 percent of their time strategically. Nonetheless, Leaders are responsible for the crafting and execution of strategy and must pay attention to both.

3. *Cascade the Strategy*

When leaders meet, they often ask their subordinates to prepare information. This has a cascading effect as staff members pay attention to what their boss pays attention to. In addition, any follow-up actions from the reviews have a similar impact.

4. *Keep the Strategy on the Radar*

You would think this should be redundant. If leaders are responsible for strategy and its execution, then it seems logical that this is what they will spend most of their time doing. But as we all know, this is not the case. Leaders are distracted by both internal and external issues: product launches, staff turnover, e-mail, conference calls, new products from the competition, market movement, stock price, and others. These succeed in distracting leaders from the laser beam focus they should have on implementing the new strategy.

5. *Focus on Solving the Strategic Problems*

By meeting every two weeks, leaders keep their attention on solving the big picture, so they are not distracted by operational issues. Leaders are easily distracted by such issues because they think they can help with them, and it feels good. But that is not what they are being paid for. When they get together at the two-week meeting they must report progress made. This helps keep them focused on the big picture and ensure they delegate the operational issues.

Three Principles of a Good Review

Three principles characterize good reviews:

- Transparency in the implementation—leaders and staff members share developments freely. Information reported in the reviews must be grounded and have clarity. The content must be accurate, useful, and timely. Reviews must be open and frank to be efficient, and effective, and drive the implementation forward.

- Confidence in numbers—the reviews are both quantitative and qualitative. It is critical that the numbers reported are accurate and that any assumptions made are upfront.
- Responsibility for taking action—a key purpose of SIR is to ensure that those responsible are taking action.

The Red Arrows, the famous U.K. pilot team, believe that after every flight together, they should sit down and discuss their performance using the following guidelines:

- Be honest.
- Create an atmosphere where people are comfortable enough to admit mistakes.
- Video everything to analyze everything.
- The leader critiques himself first.

As well as ensuring that the right actions and behaviors are being taken, the two-week meetings also identify unanticipated problems—which will occur, as implementation never goes according to plan. What is planned in the war room is never what happens on the battlefield. This is because there are too many factors that influence strategy. Customer expectations change, as do markets and the competition. Internally, there will always be staff turnover, operational issues, and new challenges to overcome. It is therefore critical that leaders closely monitor the implementation and address unanticipated problems as they arise.

Implementation without proper review is like the man falling from a 30-story building. At each floor, someone asks him how he is doing and he replies, "So far looking good!"

The core of the Weight Watchers approach is the weekly meeting that promotes weight loss through education and group support, in conjunction with a flexible, healthy diet. Each week, 1.5 million people attend approximately 50,000 Weight Watchers meetings, led by 15,000 classroom leaders around the world. In the Weight Watchers business model, the counselors talk to you, weigh you, and educate you through group involvement about food and exercise.

Procter & Gamble holds "bare knuckle" meetings. The expression is an old boxing term, from an encounter where the gloves are off. In these meetings, the best ideas are presented and discussions are hard-hitting and to the point. Even more interesting is that the whole organization is held accountable for the actions agreed on.

If you identify small problems and address them before they grow into big problems, you will stay on the right track. If you don't review implementation frequently, then you won't know what you don't know. If you do not know what is going on, how can you take corrective action?

It is habitually the small problems that cause the downfall of an implementation.

Consider the stock market crash of 1987 as a dramatic illustration of how small events can have enormous consequences. The immediate causes of the collapse were small, so small that even with the benefit of hindsight they have not been identified with any degree of confidence. Or consider that the Bear Stearns collapse can almost be attributed to a single e-mail from Goldman Sachs that leaked out and opened the floodgates. Hundreds of hedge funds and clients started yanking their investments.

As a minimum for the review, leaders need to know what the strategic objectives and goals are, what actions are being taken to achieve them, and what needs to be done differently.

Leaders must start every review by checking that the actions agreed upon in the preceding meeting are being undertaken or have been completed. It is the actions that you take every day in your business that either move you closer to your strategy or further away.

No plan survives contact with the enemy.
                                            —Colonel Tom Kolditz

---

This is the global best practice among CEOs that goes a furthest to ensure the successful implementation of a strategy. In "Why CEOs Fail," Ram Charan and Geoff Calvin indicated that one best practice of leading CEOs occurs at the start of every meeting.[1] Successful CEOs follow up from the preceding meeting and make sure that actions have been taken. Not very glamorous—but it is effective.

Implementation is all about demonstrating and taking the right behaviors and actions, and leaders are primarily responsible for ensuring that staff members are demonstrating and taking the right behaviors and actions.

Summary—Leaders' Role in Implementation

Two things leaders must do differently:

1. **Conduct two-week strategy reviews.**
   Make sure that the strategy is fully reviewed every three months by breaking it down into small components that can be reviewed every two weeks.

   Every two weeks, a strategy review is conducted to ensure the right actions and behaviors are being taken. The meetings are used by the leadership to identify and overcome any unexpected problems that arise. No matter how good the planning was, the strategy will never roll out as expected, as there are too many variables that impact its implementation.

   These are the key benefits of the leadership team meeting every two weeks to discuss strategy implementation:

   - Demonstrate to the whole organization the importance of the new strategy.
   - Change the dialogue among leaders from talking mostly about operational issues to talking about strategic issues.
   - Cascade the strategy through the organization.
   - Keep the strategy on the leaders' radar.
   - Solve the strategic problems that are the leaders' proper concern.

2. **Resolve small problems before they become big problems.**
   The reviews help identify small problems before they become large problems, and also ensure that leaders know how the implementation is performing. In the past, leaders have delegated the responsibility for the implementation without following through. The review keeps leaders up to date and allows them to corrective action when necessary.

A global best practice among CEOs is to start every review by checking that the actions agreed upon in the last meeting are being executed.

Endnote

1 Ram Charan and Geoffrey Colvin, "Why CEOs Fail: It's rarely for lack of smarts or vision. Most unsuccessful CEOs stumble because of one simple, fatal shortcoming," *Fortune,* June 21, 1999, p. 68; accessed at http://money.cnn.com/magazines/fortune/fortune_archive/1999/06/21/261696/index.htm, May 10, 2009.

CONCLUSION

Six Necessary Mind Shifts
for Implementing Strategy

The revival of the computer giant wasn't due to vision, fixing IBM was all about execution.

—Louis Gerstner, former CEO of IBM

My interviews with leaders who successfully executed their strategies reveal that at some point, they dramatically changed the way they thought about implementation. A mind shift occurred. From the research and our work with clients, Bridges has extracted six mind shifts that need to take place for implementation to be successful, contradicting much traditional literature on the subject. I describe these new required mind shifts as a conclusion to the main text, noting the old mind-set in quotation marks.

Mind Shift #1—"When crafting strategy is complete, the hardest part is over." No, implementation is twice as difficult as crafting strategy.

For decades, business leaders have quite rightly focused on developing a strategy for change. Business schools teach the importance of strategy and how to create the right one for an organization's needs. The leaders' role is to design that strategy. The consequence, however, is that once leaders have created their strategies, they believe they have completed most of their responsibilities. The hardest part is over. They habitually underestimate the challenge of implementing strategy. Many delegate it to others, taking their eyes off what needs to be done to put the strategy in place.

Bridges research indicates that implementing strategy is at least *twice as hard* as crafting the right strategy. The fact that 9 out of 10 implementations fail supports this statement. They fail not because the strategy was wrong, but because of poor implementation.

Evidence to support this conclusion continues to grow. Research spanning 16 years at Newcastle University in the U.K. concluded that "business success is governed more by how well strategies are implemented than how good the strategy is to begin with." A frequently quoted *Fortune* article from June 1999 stated that companies fail to successfully implement strategy not because of bad strategy but bad execution.[1] Bridges research over the last eight years shows that 9 out of 10 strategies fail to be implemented successfully.

When I ask leaders in the seminars I run in 35 cities if they would prefer to have a good strategy implemented badly or a bad strategy implemented well, they vote for a good strategy implemented badly. If you agree—if you believe that having the right strategy means you are moving in the right direction or have the foundation from which to build—well, that is the wrong answer. It is more important for organizations to be good at implementation. If they have in place the tools, systems, techniques, and abilities to realize that the strategy is not working, they can go upstream when required and make the necessary changes.

Consider also that no leadership team *intentionally* adopts a bad strategy. It is only in the course of execution that leaders realize that the strategy is not performing. By being good at implementation, organizations will be able to read the signs and make the necessary changes. It is the *implementation* of a strategy that delivers revenue, not the crafting.

The time has come in the evolution of strategy to move from just focusing on the crucial question on how to develop a strategy to also look at how to implement it.

Mind Shift #2—"Most people resist change." No, most people are open to change when it is communicated in the right way.

Contrary to popular belief, most people do not resist change! This is probably the most controversial of the six mind shifts, because for years we have firmly believed that most staff members will resist change. Keep in mind that if currently prevailing beliefs are accurate, implementation efforts would not be failing so frequently. The question of why people mistakenly believe staff members resist change and its implications are critical to successful implementation.

From its research, Bridges discovered that when a new strategy is launched, staff members generally respond in one of four ways: indifference, resistance, disbelief, and support. The response depends on what the change means to the individual.

Consider these research statistics:

- Twenty percent (and only 20 percent) do resist change. And these resisters tend to complain about anything and everything. They badmouth the implementation behind the leaders' backs, complaining that the money could be spent better on bonuses instead of a "lost cause" like this. They try to convince those around them that this strategy is just another management fad. Based on these characteristics, we call such people saboteurs. If their views win out, the whole implementation fails. You can probably identify one or two saboteurs in your organization!

- Sixty percent of the staff members are fence-sitters, neither supporting the implementation nor opposing it. They arrive at 9 AM and depart at 7 PM. In between, they simply do their jobs. They don't volunteer for additional work, but they don't actively resist change either. Based on these characteristics, we call them groupies. They like safety in numbers.

- Twenty percent welcome the change, embrace it, and willingly support it. They become the early adopters who drive the change. Based on these characteristics, we call them mavericks.

There is also one last group who are not easy to spot because they are hidden among the saboteurs. Based on their characteristics, we call them double agents. They initially resist, but can become mavericks over time. Double agents have seen change many times before and doubt that the new strategy will succeed. They have also been called to arms too often and have witnessed too many failures. Double agents start out acting like saboteurs, but once they conclude that this implementation is the 1 in 10 that will succeed, they get on board, becoming supportive and active mavericks.

So why is it commonly believed that people resist change? Poor communication—most leaders fail to present the Biz Case for effective change. They present why the organization must change, but not why individuals must change and what they expect staff members to do differently.

Within the four groups, saboteurs make the most noise. As a result, they create the largest commotion and lead others to the wrong impression that most people resist change. Groupies keep quiet because they do not want to draw attention to themselves. Mavericks just get on with the work on hand.

Leaders must shift their beliefs and communicate the right message. Only then will they develop the right people policies for addressing implementation.

Mind Shift #3—"It's all about taking action." No, it's about taking the *right* action.

Every organization takes action and fills up the amount of time it has with activity. Is the action, however, moving it closer to its strategy or further away? The difference between success and failure is that successful leaders drive the right action. They know what needs to be done throughout the organization on a daily basis, and ensure that staff members are not just busy, they are doing the work *today* that will deliver the planned strategy *tomorrow*.

In Chapter 2, I introduced the Implementation Compass, Bridges Business Consultancy's proprietary tool, as a way for leaders to identify the right actions to implement strategy. The tool contains the eight best practices of organizations that successfully execute strategy, and this is what we use with our clients.

As an example, when a large software company rolled out its global strategy in the Asia-Pacific region, the right action initially was to convince people why change was needed when the company was doing so well. This is called the Biz Case. This company rolled out a teaser campaign that ignited interest and curiosity in its new strategy, starting the implementation the right way.

A Middle East bank created its new strategy but did not have a common understanding among its leaders. So the strategy planners developed a strategy map to translate the new plan into specific objectives. They also developed measures that ensured the leadership team and staff members were all on the same page.

A local government division wanted to improve its back-office operations to support its new strategy. The division leaders required staff members to engage at two levels. First, all staff members were trained on how to map their work and identify improvements within their own scope. Second, key staff members were asked to participate in cross-functional process redesigns using the DMAIC (Define, Measure, Analyze, Improve, and Control—from Six Sigma) approach. Rolling out the strategy included making sure that staff members tuned in to both "radio stations": WIII-FM (What Is In It For Me) and WIEX-FM (What Is Expected From Me).

Mind Shift #4—"Communication is all about making sure people understand the strategy." No, staff members also must know exactly what action they need to take and be motivated to take it.

Before staff members can adopt a new strategy, they must first understand it. Absolutely. Successful implementation, however, goes beyond ensuring staff members *understand* the strategy; they must also know what to do and be motivated to do it.

Most current communication about a new strategy focuses on the launch, which is usually marked with electronic presentations, briefings, and T-shirts. Shifting the focus from the initial fanfare to the day-to-day work of embracing the strategy is imperative.

The communication must also spell out what each staff member needs to do differently as a result of the new strategy. The question "What actions should I take to participate in the new strategy?" has to be answered for everyone. And there's more. Ways to motivate those who implement the strategy (staff members, not leaders) must be introduced. Measures to track the new strategy need to be set up. New behaviors need to be encouraged through reinforcement. Early adopters should be recognized and encouraged so others follow their lead.

When Rolls Royce rolled out its new strategy a few years ago, it used "strategy storyboards" to share the new message across its broad organization. The storyboards translated abstract ideas into concrete actions. They not only explained why the strategy was important, they showed what Rolls Royce staff members were expected to do differently. In addition, 75 managers were trained to conduct the briefing and hold at least 4,000 presentations around the world. After this effort, staff members were able to both understand the strategy and know exactly what to do to help implement it.

Leaders must realize that strategy can't be implemented if it can't be understood, and it can't be understood if it can't be broken down into action steps. While strategy is designed at the top of the organization chart, it gets implemented from the bottom up. Effective communication fills the gap and brings the two together.

Mind Shift #5—"What worked yesterday will work tomorrow." No, new strategies are needed approximately every two years.

Leaders have had the habit of extending yesterday's performance when planning for tomorrow, as they used to be able to rely on a strategy for 8 to 10 years. Those days are long gone.

Today, many organizations (depending on their industry and product) plan strategy for only two or three years. The cycle of change occurs more and more frequently. As a result, you can no longer depend on yesterday's model for success; you must implement a new strategy more frequently than ever before.

On the Standard & Poor's list in 1985, 35 percent of the companies were considered high risk (that is, their probability of achieving long-term, stable earnings growth was low). In the 2006 list, that figure had risen to 73 percent. In another indicator, from 1973 to 1983, 35 percent of those companies listed in the Fortune 1000 were new. From 1983 to 1993, 45 percent of the Fortune 1000 companies were new, and from 1993 to 2003, 60 percent of them were new.

One company comfortable with constant change is Google, which provides various Internet services. The company has built a culture that not only allows its change-friendly people to adapt easily, but it has also become the number one company that people want to work for in the United States. Google receives more than 3,000 job applications a day. This is hardly surprising, as the working conditions on the "Googleplex" headquarters campus are some of the best in the world, and the company holds 64 percent of the market share in its category. In its first 10 years, Google created more investor wealth in less time than any other company in history—US$10.6 billion in revenue earned.

As noted in Chapter 7, the late management guru Peter Drucker observed that "maintaining yesterday is difficult and time-consuming and therefore always commits the institution's scarcest and most valuable resources—and above all, its ablest people—to non-results."[2] Acting this way means your people are not available to create a successful tomorrow.

Mind Shift #6—"Strategy implementation must be reviewed twice a year." No, it must be reviewed twice a month—at least!

In many management meetings, Bridges research has revealed, 85 percent of leaders' time is spent on operational issues while 15 percent is spent on strategic issues. However, leaders are not meant to solve day-to-day problems (though they do so because it feels good and they can do it)—they are responsible for crafting and implementing strategy.

An indicator that an organization is on the right path to implement its strategy is when the ratio is reversed. That is, when 85 percent of the leaders' time is spent on strategic issues and 15 percent on operational issues.

Changing strategy means changing the dialogue and agenda at your meetings, and specifically at your management meetings. Once it is successfully changed, the effect will cascade through the organization. Immediate reports pay attention to what bosses pay attention to.

The catalyst for this dialogue change is frequently scheduled strategy reviews. If leaders are responsible for both crafting and executing strategy, doesn't it follow that implementation should be discussed as frequently as possible?

During reviews, you are not analyzing the whole strategy. Rather, you break it down into small chunks. This means that in the course of every quarter, the strategy is reviewed in its entirety.

To predict where an organization will be in two years, do not look at its strategy paper. Instead, pay attention to the daily actions its leaders and staff members take.

A Final Word

I hope, however, that I have planted a seed of doubt, and that your thinking will begin to grow and change as a result of reading this book and pondering your own experiences.

Endnotes

1 Ram Charan and Geoffrey Colvin, "Why CEOs Fail: It's rarely for lack of smarts or vision. Most unsuccessful CEOs stumble because of one simple, fatal shortcoming," *Fortune*, June 21, 1999, p. 68; accessed at http://money. cnn.com/magazines/fortune/fortune_archive/1999/06/21/261696/index.htm, May 10, 2009.

2 e-BIM Editorial Staff, "Abandoning the Obsolete and Unproductive: A Difficult but Necessary Task," November 17, 2008. http://www.sixsigmaiq.com/ Columnarticle.cfm?externalID=387&ColumnID=11

BRIDGES BUSINESS CONSULTANCY INT.

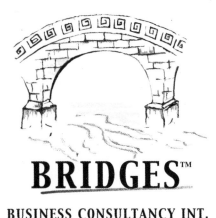

BRIDGES™

BUSINESS CONSULTANCY INT.

Welcome to Bridges Business Consultancy Int., a pioneer in the field of strategy implementation. Bridges was founded at the start of the millennium to research, develop, and integrate strategy implementation in businesses. It is our laser beam focus and we work with governments, multinational organizations, and local businesses in five continents to assist the execution of their strategy.

For eight years we have researched strategy implementation and discovered that leaders constantly fail to deliver to their staff members, Board, and shareholders on the promises of a new strategy 90 percent of the time. Bridges has been working ferociously to reverse this statistic.

Our research has focused on identifying what the 1 in 10 who implement strategy successfully do right, and developing tools and techniques to support leaders. A key conclusion has been that strategy execution lacks a framework. This led to the creation of the

Implementation Compass™, a framework to implement strategy. It explains the eight "directions" you need to consider.

In 2004 our CEO and founder, Robin Speculand, published the now best-selling book *Bricks to Bridges: Make Your Strategy Come Alive*. The book introduced the Implementation Compass™ and spurned our signature seminar, which now runs in more than 35 cities around the world. Various other tools and techniques have been developed to provide critical support.

Strategy implementation is not rocket science—it is common sense. Just because it is common sense, however, that does not mean it is common practice. We are here to share best practices, and at heart we are a team of people who truly believe in—and passionately focus on—strategy execution!

Bridges Consultancy's work has been featured on global and local media outlets, including the BBC Global, CNBC, *Financial Times,* and various strategy journals.

INDEX